W9-BRX-578

My Corner of New England

Thoughts on nature and human nature from a Pilgrim House on Cape Cod Bay

My Corner of New England

by Robert M. Bartlett

Illustrations by Jan Norton

Peter E. Randall
PUBLISHER

Peter E. Randall Publisher
Post Office Box 4726
Portsmouth, New Hampshire 03801

Acknowledgements: Music in the Air and Ballet Dancers of the Sea first appeared in *Neapolitan Magazine*, Naples, Florida and are used in revised form by permission. Portions of Friendly Voices of the Night and Oysterin' were published in the *Christian Science Monitor*. Parts of Ballet Dancers of the Sea were published in *Field and Stream*, part of One for the Blackbird in the *Boston Globe* and a portion of Broad Margin of Leisure in *Readers Digest*.

The author is grateful for the use of the following quotations: from *The Year of the Butterfly* by George Ordish, Charles Scribners Sons, from *Of Stars and Men* by Harlow Shapley, Beacon Press, from *Ships in Harbor* by David Morton, Putnam, from *Masterpieces of Religious Verse*, a poem by Mary Carolyn Davis, Harper & Row.

Library of Congress Cataloging in Publication Data

Bartlett, Robert Merrill,
    My corner of New England.

    1. Plymouth Region (Mass.) — Description and travel.
2. Natural history — Massachusetts — Plymouth Region.
3. Bartlett, Robert Merrill,   . I. Title.
F74.P8B37   1984   974.4'82   84-2170
ISBN 0-914-339-05-2

4

TO my wife,
    Sue
        my inspiration
            collaborator
                editor

Other Books by Robert M. Bartlett

The Faith Of The Pilgrims
The Pilgrim Way
Thanksgiving Day
They Stand Invincible: Men Who Are Reshaping Our World
With One Voice: Prayers From Around The World
Sky Pioneer: The Story of Igor I. Sikorsky
They Dared To Live
They Did Something About It
They Work For Tomorrow
They Dared To Believe
Discovery: A Guidebook In Living
A Boy's Book Of Prayers
The Ascending Trail
Christian Conquests
Pilgrim Robert Bartlett
The Fifth Race
Builders Of A New World
The Great Empire Of Silence
Pilgrim House By The Sea
The Life Of Y. C. James Yen

Credo of a Naturalist

If, therefore, the Maker of all things, who had done nothing without design, had furnished this earthy globe, like a museum, with the most admirable proof of his wisdom and power; if, moreover, this splendid theater would be adorned in vain without a spectator; and if he placed in it Man, the chief and most perfect of all his works, that he may observe in them the evident mark of divine wisdom:

Thus we learn not only from the opinion of moralists and divines, but also from the testimony of nature herself, that this world is destined to the celebration of the Creator's glory, and that man is placed in it to be the publisher and interpreter of the wisdom of God; and indeed he who does not make himself acquainted with God from the consideration of nature, would scarcely acquire knowledge of him from any other source; for 'If we have no faith in things which are seen, how should we believe those things which are not seen?'

Carolus Linnaeus
1707-1780

Contents

Foreword

There must be something to the tradition about the heritage of the soil. I come from a line of ministers and educators who were gardeners. No doubt it was partly economic necessity, as well as romantic attachment, that led them to cultivate fruits, vegetables and flowers. Grandfather Bartlett left his Pilgrim roots in New England to seek knowledge at Oberlin College where he won three degrees and taught Greek. He moved on to Maryville College in Tennessee and spent his life as college pastor and professor of Greek and Hebrew, enjoying the big brick house on the campus and his orchard and garden.

My father graduated from there. He studied theology and then served as a Presbyterian minister in the Midwest. He cherished his Massachusetts heritage but was never able to return East to reestablish family connections. He gave me a book on the Bartlett genealogy which included a picture of the homestead in Plymouth. "I hope you will go back some day and see the place," he said.

I followed in his footsteps to Maryville College. There I met Sue, who came from a Texas family—descendants of the Jamestown Colony who were pioneers in shaping the Lone Star State—all of them lovers of the soil. We both transferred to Oberlin College where the New England ties were strong. After graduation we were married in the Oberlin College Church. I was drawn to Yale Divinity School. Enamored by the romance of China, we set out for the Orient as soon as I received my graduate degree and spent three years teaching in Yenching University in Peking. On our return, I was called to a Congregational Church in Norwood, a suburb of Boston. We were in love with the New England seacoast and glad to be able to explore the country.

An aged cousin, widowed and without children, died in the old Plymouth house and through good fortune we became the owners in 1935 of that ancient dwelling pictured in the genealogy book given me by my father. Built in 1660 by Pilgrim Robert Bartlett, it had never been out of the Barlett line.

It was a gray shingled, gambrel roof house with three acres on a country road in South Plymouth. Small farming was still going on in the area. There was plenty of open woodland for hiking and quail hunting, a brook and pond for fishing and good neighbors, close enough but not too close. The property was in sad shape. The day we took possession we cleared away an overgrown clump of rugosa roses which blocked the front door. We spent many summers of labor and a good deal of money, borrowed from the Five Cent Savings Bank, in restoring the house.

We took to the soil that very first spring, plowing and planting almost all the vegetables in the catalog. We set out a sizable orchard and many rare trees and flowering shrubs. The old house perked up in the midst of this support from nature, with the explosion of leaf and flower and in companionship with the gracious sentinels that took up their posts about her, offering their shade and perfume in tribute to the dwelling that had stood for nearly three hundred years on this spot chosen by the Pilgrims.

All our summers were spent here. Spring, fall and winter the place welcomed us when we could slip away from professional responsibilities for a respite. With a forced hot air heating system, we needed only to push the thermometer up or down on coming and going. We talked before an open fire about my predecessors who walked the wide board floors and cooked over the big fireplace, roasting wild fowl and baking bread in the Dutch oven. Since retirement, this has been our only home.

The growing of flowers and the study of birds and the natural environment have been my lifelong interests and recreation. I have recorded some of these pleasant experiences in this book.

Robert M. Bartlett
Plymouth, Massachusetts

Legacy

A Goodly Heritage

It was a humiliating experience that day in the elementary school in a small Missouri town when the boys ganged up on me. The year was 1905. It was the opening day in September and I was entering the first grade, dressed in keeping with the importance of the occasion in the suit mother had ordered from Best & Company in New York. It was a navy blue sailor suit, long pants and a middy blouse with a round flat hat to match, a black and gold band around it. At my tender age I did not surmise that I might appear like a Beau Brummell in a small town in the corn belt.

Mother held to high standards. She loved pretty clothes and flowery hats. She was a musician and an advocate of culture and decorum. Her doctor father in Tennessee took her to Nashville when she was sixteen and bought her a wardrobe of fashionable dresses, hats and shoes. She could not maintain her style on father's meager salary but she pinched pennies to order garments from Best's for her four children once a year.

The local lads had never seen a sailor outfit straight from Fifth Avenue. As soon as we broke for recess they gathered around me and taunted me. One aggressive chap grabbed my pancake hat and, with a mighty swoop, sailed it up onto the tile roof of our two story, red brick schoolhouse. That was an interminable recess and morning session. I ran home for lunch and divested myself of that naval uniform and never wore it again. It ended up in a church barrel for the Presbyterian Mission in Peking.

Father and mother both admired the heritage that had been passed on to them from the Pilgrims and Puritans. Father dressed frugally, by necessity, but always with dignity. He never appeared in public except in a gray or black suit, white shirt and dark tie. He took after his professor father whose photograph presents the mien of a scholar with beautifully groomed hair and goatee. He honored his inheritance of learning. He had studied Hebrew and Greek under his father. He worked faithfully on the sermons he delivered each Sunday to his congregation. He wrote them in long hand with pen and ink and kept them in neat folders with their dates of delivery. He read them over in his study, pacing the room, repeating them word for word and seldom looked at his manuscript in the pulpit. His standards would not permit him to slump into easy and indifferent habits of scholarship. His parish was a cross-section of a Midwest town, far from a college or any intellectual stimulant, a market center for a rural area built around the Santa Fe Railroad shops.

Most of the townspeople and members of the church liked father for his warm, outgoing nature and ability as a public speaker, but not many appreciated his knowledge of the Bible, history and literature. However, he never gave up trying to widen their horizons. Occasionally he would present a weekday lecture in the church. I heard him once on Julius Caesar, "The Tall Man of the Tiber." He wrote it carefully, with all historic sources noted, and gave it with more than classroom skill. He appeared in his stiff-bosom shirt and collar, black four-in-hand tie, black cutaway and striped trousers. It was an effort to inspire his listeners to reach out for more knowledge.

At least it worked with one lad in the sparse audience. I caught something from his story of ancient Rome that encouraged me to be a seeker. I listened to a lecture that he gave on Oliver Cromwell, which was my introduction to the Puritans and their contribution to America. He liked to tackle giants of history like John Huss, John Calvin and Martin Luther.

The manse was a modest red brick with four bedrooms and an expansive front porch. The church, a short walk away, was a mongrel stone structure with a square, squat tower. The walls and ceiling were a bilious buff tone. The pews were circular. On the platform was the central pulpit, dark walnut with shiny veneer finish. In back of the clergy chairs was the choir loft and its overpowering display of organ pipes. Windows blocked the sunlight with imitation Tiffany glass panes of blue, green and amber.

Father took the lead in trying to unite the Northern Presbyterians and the Cumberland Presbyterians. The animosities of the Civil War lingered in this area of Missouri. There was heated controversy between the mergerites and the anti-mergerites. Some of the Cumberland people talked openly about running him out of town. I once dreamed that they were plotting to assassinate him.

He kept a garden in the back yard or on a vacant lot nearby, raising vegetables for a family of six. He could be found there early in the morning and in the evening. Gardening offered him exercise and relaxation. I can taste even now, the luscious, warm tomatoes that I pulled off the vine and ate on the spot. The garden was his refuge.

In those days, Social Security was undreamed of, as were unemployment benefits and cost of living raises. Security in our household meant faith that the Lord would provide. If father received a two dollar honorarium for a funeral or wedding, mother might get a new Easter bonnet, but more likely the money would go for a pair of shoes or toward the back grocery bill.

If the going was hard, the church treasury low, or he had faced an abrasive session with a troublesome elder, that evening he would get out his violin. My mother, who had studied at the New England Conservatory of Music, accompanied him at the upright piano. They played and sang all their favorite songs and hymns, usually ending with:

O God, beneath thy guiding hand
Our exiled fathers crossed the sea,
And when they trod the wintry strand,
With prayer and psalm they worshiped thee.
Laws, freedom, truth and faith in God

Came with those exiles o'er the waves,
And where their Pilgrim feet have trod,
The God they trusted guards their graves.

I would hear them singing from my bedroom upstairs where I was studying Latin verbs and I vowed that when I grew up I would visit that Pilgrim land. I never dreamed then that I would one day own the ancestral home and live in it for forty-nine years.

Horse Sense

Attics are repositories for cradles, trunks, scrap bags of quilt squares, grandmother's rocker, discarded toys, possibly a valuable antique or a lively bit of family history, hidden among records and newspaper clippings in a leather-bound box with iron clasps and lined with wallpaper.

Time has a way of dispersing family treasures and memories, but there is usually something tragic or romantic to be found in old attics, especially when the occupants have been in the same family for many generations. New Englanders never throw anything away and that is why there are so many antiques in this part of the country.

The owners of our house, through the decades, had done what we all do. They tried to keep up with the times. They added the comforts and conveniences they could afford. There were single electric bulbs hanging from the ceilings in the downstairs rooms. A pot-bellied stove was installed in the parlor fireplace and a soapstone sink and hand pump in the keeping room. Discarded articles were stored for future use.

Our small attic under the eaves of the gambrel roof really set us back in time. It has an eighteen-inch square window and we used a kerosene lamp in our first exploration of its contents. A shoe box containing eight pieces of a Liverpool mug, evidently valued by someone, each piece carefully wrapped in newspaper, was our first discovery. We took it to the Boston Museum of Fine Arts where it was restored to perfection by a young man who was a master in this amazing art. It now is on our keeping room mantel.

Newspapers and magazines we faithfully scanned, casting away most of them. A spinning wheel was brought downstairs and set by the bedroom fireplace. Scrap bags we gave to a neighbor who makes quilts. A flower picture, made of the hair of all Bartletts then living in the area, arranged in an oval frame, Sue gave to a Bartlett cousin. She has now been dead some years, and the other day Sue asked her daughter where the picture was. She said she had put it in the attic. Her mother had liked it and knew whose hair was in each flower. But it gave her the shivers. Sue agreed. We never cared for that kind of memorabilia.

A leather-bound box, referred to above, yielded revealing stories about my ancestors and a trait of Pilgrim character I call "horse sense." Some previous family historian had appreciated these facts and copied them from the Town Records into his diary.

The first one was about Mercy Bartlett, youngest daughter of Robert and Mary Warren Bartlett. At age eighteen, she and a girl friend were involved in a slight scandal. The records of October 25, 1668 state:

James Clarke complaineth against Sarah Barlow and Marcye Bartlett, in an action of slaunder and defamation, to the damage of two hundred pounds for reporting that they saw the said James Clarke kisse his mayde, and use other uncuiell carriages that hee acted towards her in the field uppon the Lords day.

This was refered to be ended by the majestrates by mutuall consent of each of the pties, whose determination and judgment is as followeth:

In reference to the complaint of James Clarke against Sarah Barlow and Marcye Bartlett, for defaneing him in makeing report of unseemly familiarities between him and his mayde, the Court, having fully considered the matter, and

compared the testimony relateing thereunto, and takeing notice how the pties that have charged him have, one or both of them, said and unsaid or greatly varyed in their relations about it, doe declare, that we judge they have defamed and slaundered him therein, because the things charged by them doth in noe measure appear by testimonie; and also their way of devoulging it was manifestly scanderlous, although there had bine some appaerances of truth in theire report, and therefore for this theire misdemenor doe amerce them ten shillings appece to the King (On the margin). This was non suited because that the said Marcye Bartlett was found under couert barud.

This incident offers a remarkable insight into the discernment of the Pilgrims. The girls were scolded for gossiping and levied a small fine to suggest punishment, but the fine was not collected. James Clarke suffered public embarrassment (and no doubt a scolding from his wife). And that was that. What amazes me is that the girls did not go into hysterics and whip up a witch hunt as the teenagers in Salem did. This does not sound like the stern Puritanism, so erroneously attributed to the Pilgrims. Although there might have been a mild commotion in the Bartlett house, the family appears to have rallied behind Mercy and this tempest in a teapot was treated as such.

The diary continued with an exposé of witchcraft (which was raging all over the "civilized world" at that time). Dinah Sylvester charged Mrs. William Holmes with witchcraft May 7, 1661. Her husband sued for slander. The case was brought before Governor Thomas Prence and his Board of Assistants.

"Whatever do you have to support your charge?" Dinah Sylvester was asked.

"She appeared to me as a witch," she answered.

"In what shape?"

"In the shape of a bear."

"How far away was the bear?"

"About a stone's throw from the path."

"What manner of tail did the bear have?"

"I could not tell as the head was towards me . . ."

I can see the members of the Board holding back a smile as they asked their questions.

"But the plot was too shallow, and whatever there was of Deviltry in it was thrown upon the one who made the Attempt."

Dinah Sylvester was found guilty of slander and ordered to pay Mrs. Holmes five pounds and to openly confess her error and repay costs and charges. Unlike the Bay Colony, there was never a witch hunt in Plymouth.

The most amazing incident in the records, illustrating Pilgrim balance and judgment, deals with the thorny area of theological disputation. In 1638, the Reverend Charles Chauncy became minister of the Plymouth church. He was an ardent believer in baptism by immersion. Members were accustomed to the more universal baptism by christening. Moreover, the water in Plymouth is never warm, even in summer, so there was considerable dissension.

The ministers of the Bay Colony were asked to try to set Chauncy straight and ease the conflict, but they failed. Governor Bradford smoothed the troubled waters by stating that parents wishing to have their children immersed could use Chauncy and those who preferred sprinkling could use the Reverend John Rayner who was the teacher of the congregation.

So that crisis was settled without further wrangling. And Chauncy journeyed, by a devious path, to become the second president of Harvard College after promising that he would avoid the subject of immersion. Their president, Henry Dunster, had been dismissed because of a disputation over baptism.

As I laid down the yellowed sheets of the journal, written in a fine hand, but in fading ink, I was refreshed to find this account of horse sense in the early records of America. Would that there could be a renaissance of this simple, basic virtue in Washington, Boston, Plymouth and in every hamlet in the land.

Ponds and Hills

When it comes to square miles, Plymouth is the largest town in Massachusetts, spreading along the Atlantic some twenty miles toward the Cape Cod Canal. "America's Home Town" also boasts 365 ponds, one for each day in the year, ranging from four to 400 acres in size. It is a surprise to find these jewels of fresh water so close to the ocean. There are names like Bloody Pond, Boot Pond, Gallows Pond, Clam Pudding Pond, Halfway Pond, Ship Pond, Rabbit Pond and Great Herring Pond.

Each of these creations of nature is a small world in itself with its own display of scrub pine, oak, maple and willow, wild roses, blueberries, cat-tails, mallow, water lilies, pickerel weed, iris and loosestrife. There are fish, frogs, dragon flies, turtles, muskrats, song birds, gulls, quails and partridges.

On Halfway Island, in Halfway Pond, is a little fragment of New England's Garden of Eden, protected by foresighted owners who controlled the island for generations. We find stands of oak, beech, birch and pine, which give us a picture of how Plymouth forests may have looked in 1620. Here also are shrubs and flowers that have disappeared from the rest of the area.

Nature generously tossed in a supply of brooks and rivers to protect and care for these inland lakes. Jones River to the north, named after the captain of the *Mayflower,* Town Brook, Eel River, Bartlett Brook and Indian Brook. These little streams have furnished passage for the alewives to their inland spawning areas and to wend their way back to salt water. They also carry off the flood water from the cranberry bogs and help regulate the complex water system that was developed aeons ago.

The glacial era, as it bade farewell to New England, left us an assortment of level land, hills, valleys, hollows, kettles, dips and depressions, where water collected to form our ponds. No wonder that these havens, set back from the highways and protected by forests of pine, are now spotted by cabins of summer people as well as homes of year-round residents. Most of the ponds are closed to motorboats and one may enjoy a refreshing dip or fish for perch, bass and pickerel.

Early explorers commented on the Plymouth environment. Captain John Smith, in 1611, called it "the paradise of these parts." Martin Pring wrote of his voyage to the New World in 1603, describing New England as "a land of God's good blessing." Robert Cushman, in 1621, praised Plymouth's "dales and meadow ground, full of rivers and sweet springs." William Bradford and Edward Winslow noted the primeval forests, the clean streams and ponds, the abundance of fish, wild fowl, nuts and berries.

The Pilgrims were conscious, in those early years, of the need for conservation. They passed a law in 1626 to control the exporting of timber out of the colony without consent of the governor and his council. They restricted the clearing of land by fire and injuring the trees by improper cutting. They, likewise, made laws to protect the salt water fish supply and the alewives in Town Brook in order to help them in their upstream journey to the ponds.

Pilgrim leaders appreciated the aid the rivers and ponds offered. Town Brook, with its water power, furnished the site of Stephen Deane's corn mill in 1623 and John Jenny's grist mill in 1636. Along this peaceful brook New England's earliest industries were established: fulling mills, forges, leather mills and cotton mills. The ponds provided bog iron which led to the building of blast furnaces that made Plymouth County the iron center of the colonies for a time. There were eight blast furnaces in Carver.

Measured against the sweep of time and the forces of change wrought by sun, wind, rain and man, I realize that the ponds may not be as they are forever. So it is with the brooks and the rivers. We also have a share in their demise. We are contributing to their absorption into bog and marshland by our disregard of the rules nature has laid down. If we overstep, in our carelessness and greed, we can hasten the departure of these fair and sweet waters where we have watched the silken wings of dragon flies resting on the bobbing typha, reflected in the sparkling shallows.

Real estate promoters now advertise Plymouth as the fastest growing town in the state, with the lowest tax rate, offering the benefits of pond and ocean and the heritage of the forefathers. The bulldozers are enjoying a heyday of prosperity as they dig cellar holes, ditches for septic tanks and uproot trees to lay out lawns and driveways. Some ponds, like Bartlett Pond, are struggling for their lives against the onslaught of sewage, chemicals and construction. Ideally located on the ocean's edge, it is rapidly filling up with weeds and muck. It is only a matter of time and the once living pond will be a marsh.

It was in the dim, prehistoric past that the Pine Hills, running along the shore from Plymouth about five miles southward, were created. Natives claim that they form the highest point on the coastline between Boston and Florida. The old, narrow Route 3 (now 3A) winds its perilous way through them. The Pine Hills are neighbors of our land. We have walked in them many times, picking wild blueberries, scouting among the glacial boulders for a weathered, brownish stone to place on our cemetery lot, and glimpsing now and then the cobalt blue of the limitless Atlantic.

During the past three summers, we have faced an invasion of gypsy moth caterpillars throughout the Pine Hills. In 1982 they staged an all-out blitz, stripping the trees bare. The caterpillars crept into our churchyard and made a shambles of all the oaks. They even ate the maples. In a few hours the cemetery was forlorn. We checked the flowering shrubs on our family lot and found that the slimy gray worms that clung to the bark of the trees had not touched them.

Within a month after the devastation, the oaks and maples had put forth a new stand of foliage. This renaissance spread through the desolation of the Pine Hills. To me it was an amazing demonstration of the restorative power of nature. It is estimated that each year a tree can remake ninety percent of its living cells. During one season, a large tree can produce several million leaves.

The hills stand as symbols of endurance. The burned derelicts left by recent fires are sad to see, but scrub pine and oak are growing up to cover the scars. Through the passage of time, geologists tell me, the ponds may lose some of their beauty or even disappear. But the hills will endure.

A Blackfoot Indian had something to say about the permanence of the land when white men tried to buy his property:

> Our land is more valuable than your money. It will last forever. It will not even perish by the flames of fire. As long as the sun shines and the waters flow, this land will be here to give life to men and animals. It was put here for us by the Great Spirit and we cannot sell it because it does not belong to us. You can count your money and burn it within the nod of a buffalo's head, but only the Great Spirit can count the grains of sand and blades of grass of these plains.

Yankee Sapience

If I were given a brownstone mansion in New York City to live in tax free, I would decline the gift. I can think of nothing worse than being shut off from green grass, sunsets and expansive views. Cities give me claustrophobia with their concrete fortresses, belching fumes, their ghettos and crime statistics. My urban friends will counter with the exclamation: "Think of the cultural and educational advantages — theaters, operas, museums and lectures by celebrities!"

I can see and hear all these in my home in the country by the push of a button while I enjoy peace and quiet in my easy chair, with the call of the whippoorwill and the fragrance of petunias at my back door. We have our own book shelves, loaded with masterpieces, ever accessible.

I have listened to supposedly learned professors and pundits who speak an academic lingo without revealing much wisdom, which means, according to the dictionary, "knowing what is true and right and having the judgment to apply it." Small towns are not devoid of culture. Plymouth has a good library, study clubs, a town symphony, musical concerts, art exhibitions, a bird observatory and half a dozen museums.

Deacon Barnes was a well digger, plumber and carpenter, a resourceful workman who could turn his hand at almost any job, and a good neighbor as long as he lived. He welcomed us when we moved in. He took a look at the state of our house and gave us sound advice on how to start digging out the cellar (it was only four feet deep), on putting in bathroom and kitchen plumbing, the best kind of shingles to use on the roof and on laying out the vegetable garden.

Through the years he proved to be a man of wisdom. I enjoyed his company as much or more than some doctors of philosophy I have known. He was a wind-tanned man of the sea who loved his dory and outboard motor and took his share of flounder, tautog and cod from the bay. I often joined him, trolling for mackerel and line fishing for sole. He knew the right spots and how to coax the sputtering engine into action. He knew the winds and tides and when to come ashore if clouds threatened. He was never ruffled by a squall on the water or a tempest in the church.

Deke heard what was happening all over Plymouth and Cape Cod. He was rubbing elbows with the bigwigs and the humble as he dug wells and set up water systems. From the outset he spoke dire prophecies about the outcome of Franklin Roosevelt's "socialism." He was a self-made, pay-as-you-go individual who was for thrift in private affairs and government. "We'll never see the end of this hand-out deal," he said to me as we stopped to observe the WPA youth building a stone wall around our local cemetery. "There are six of them watching four do the work," he added.

The village minister learned to depend on Deke, who was always on hand, but never leaning too hard on his oar. He stood by his pastor when the flak was flying and eased tensions with his balance and common sense. He had two years in high school, yet he knew more about the presidents of the United States than most university graduates. He was proud of his collection of books on American history. He learned a great deal about human nature attending church and town meetings and was full of stories about local people.

We enjoyed his anecdotes about Josiah and Martha Bartlett who lived in our house before us. He did errands for them, weeded their garden and chopped their wood, not for pay, but because they were old and he "was just brought up that way." Josiah was a good fisherman, but he sometimes grew impatient with Martha who was prone to nag him to hitch up the horse and buggy and drive over the Pine Hills to Guy Cooper's General Store at Jabez Corner so she could sell some eggs and buy knitting yarn and horehound candy.

Martha was plump and good natured but Josiah was as tight as the bark on a willow tree. He kept his money in a Prince Albert tobacco can in the parlor corner cupboard. When we moved in, the can was still there but held no cash, only Martha's collection of buttons. Josiah had preceded Martha to the Great Beyond.

Deke introduced me to Guy Cooper who was the presiding genius in the old-fashioned country emporium. Guy bobbed about in and out of view amid his collection of merchandise that filled the shelves and counters and hung from walls and ceiling. There was an area for canned goods and boxed goods, sweet milk and butter-milk in glass bottles, fresh eggs in baskets, a tub of butter, jugs of molasses and a savory round of Vermont cheese with a sharp knife beside it. There were barrels of flour, sugar, dill pickles and sauer-kraut.

Garden tools were in the back and seed in bulk, where one could look a pea or bean square in the eye and calculate its potentiality. There was also a kerosene tank. A customer could fill his can and view a variety of table lamps for sale. The meat counter was the main attraction. Guy sliced the best grade of beef around. When Deke tired of mackerel and cod, he drove into town for a piece of red meat. He also bought his work shoes and overalls from Guy, who carried the real thing, with stalwart suspenders, not the skin-fitting Levis that pinch the waist and hips.

In a glass case of ribbons and trimmings, needles and thread, there were pearl-headed hat pins, pink garters with rosettes, silver vanity cases, amber side combs studded with brilliants and ivory napkin rings. The medicine section offered a variety of household remedies and sets of false teeth. At the center of the rambling building a huge potbellied iron stove was circled by wooden kegs where customers sat on cool days to chat and Guy's cronies met on wintry nights to smoke and talk politics.

If you said "charge it," Guy would write it down in one of those little books without a grunt of annoyance, even if it were a nickel's worth of candy. And one did not have to produce a social security card or a bank reference. Guy called on the phone sometimes to say that he had some prime lamb chops that day, or that Nook Farm had just brought in a bushel of fresh peas and some beautiful strawberries at twenty cents a quart. He even delivered, sending out his Ford truck to any section of town.

I enjoyed this venerable landmark for several years until Guy Cooper retired and his successor went modern. I frequently feel a nostalgia for those days as I wander about the sterile supermarket searching for a box of old-fashioned oatmeal. (All cereals today are "quick" and tasteless.) I can never find a clerk, and if I do, he doesn't know where it is either. "I don't eat the stuff," he mumbles.

I am pushed through the automatic stall like a cow being shoved into a dipping vat. There is not time to look into an inviting cracker barrel, cut a sliver of cheese, have a pickle "on the house," chat with Guy about the mackerel fishing, the east wind or the baked bean supper at the church.

Deke not only introduced me to the history of Plymouth but helped me find old wide pine floor boards and H and L hinges. When I offered to pay him for spending so much of his time counseling with us, he lifted his hand in a negative gesture. "We're neighbors," he said, "You just come over to the house some day and let me show you my president books."

Our neighbors are not the in-and-out type. They are friendly and sharing, but they keep pretty much to themselves, enjoying their own privacy and respecting others', but one knows they are always there when needed and ready to help. I would rather live among plain and caring people in a New England village than to live with the sophisticated dwellers of the skyscraper world, even in a penthouse that covers a city block and is laden with art treasures, gold bath tubs and imported flower gardens.

Those White Spires

While crossing the country by plane, I was chatting with my seat mate who asked where I lived. When I said I was from New England, he exclaimed, "Ah, the land of those white church spires." They are indeed a distinctive feature of the landscape. Driving the highways, one looks out on a panorama of hills and valleys, dotted with white church spires, supported, usually, by a colony of old colonial houses and farms.

On my way into Plymouth, I never fail to watch for the steeple of the Chiltonville Church that looms up on the west through the trees just beyond Eel River. Wherever I go, I look for these white clapboard meetinghouses that have stood on village greens for generations. They are spread to the south, the west and the north — the offspring of the Fort Meetinghouse of Plymouth.

The first winter the Pilgrims worshipped in the Common House, which they built and lost by fire. In 1623 they moved into their first church with a top deck that served as a fort to guard their plantation. In 1648, as they prospered, they dedicated a more adequate building. By that time daughter churches had sprung up as settlers moved out into the countryside: Scituate (1636), Duxbury

(1637), Barnstable (1639), Sandwich (1639), Yarmouth (1639), Taunton (1639), Marshfield (1641), Rehobeth (1645) and Eastham (1646). By 1687 eleven more were added, making a total of twenty-one Plymouth Colony communities. The first structures were rustic and unsophisticated, but in time more artistic designs appeared, rectangular in shape and ornamented by graceful spires with urns, clocks and gold leaf weathervanes, along with porticoes, pillars and clear glass mullioned windows. They were invariably painted in pristine white.

The Puritans joined the Pilgrims in this outreach toward beauty. These people were not blue-nosed ascetics. They cherished artistic furniture, pewter, silver, books, portraits and flowers. Their worship was simple. Elaborate ecclesiastical furnishings like the chancel with reredos, altar, cross and candles and a highly developed liturgy were not essential. Religion was the direct encounter of man with God. It was a matter of ideas, not forms, of teaching, not litany. However, many of the Congregational Way in recent years have added the simple chancel, altar and cross, believing that they are assets in worship.

I have visited the great cathedrals of the world and appreciate their beauty and the genius of the architects. But I find it difficult to worship God in them. The minister is too far away in an exalted pulpit. The stone floor is cold and the darkness oppressive in spite of stained glass windows. And I cannot forget the cost — years of subsistence labor that built them, more often to the glory of king and bishop than to the glory of God.

The sunlit church of the Pilgrims was organized by the people, built and paid for by the people and owned by the people. I spent twenty-two years in two of our historic New England churches, in Longmeadow and Shrewsbury, Massachusetts, both of them built before the Revolution. I marvel that the members had foresight to construct such appealing edifices. It was due in part to the heritage of learning expounded in their pulpits. Their ministers were scholars. They knew something about classic forms of architecture.

A group of settlers were granted permission to found Shrewsbury in 1717 and "to build themselves houses for forty families and settle an orthodox minister within three years." The meetinghouse was completed in 1721. Job Cushing, a graduate of Harvard, was called to be their minister. He was allowed sixty-eight pounds to build his own home on land deeded him. He was a faithful leader of the parish for nearly forty years, dropping dead while harvesting his wheat. Cushing was followed by a Yale alumnus, Joseph Sumner, a man of dignity and culture, who wore a gown and wig in the pulpit and delivered scholarly sermons to the people he served for sixty years.

The present church was built in 1766. It has a stately steeple with a gold leaf weathervane. The sanctuary, with its horseshoe balcony, double rows of shuttered windows and high paneled pulpit, with a red dossal behind it, has echoed with many sermons dealing with the tumult of the Revolution, to the Great Depression and the tornado of 1953.

Before the town hall was built, town meetings were held in the vestry, which would be packed with people ready to speak their minds on the articles in the warrant posted on the front door. Buns and gingerbread were sold at intermissions in the session that lasted for several afternoons and evenings before all items were covered.

Longmeadow was laid out on the high land above the Connecticut River just south of Springfield, and its first meetinghouse was raised in 1716. It was the religious and community center of the village. A new building was erected in 1768 on the green that reached two miles through the center of the town. It is one of the most beautiful and most photographed of the colonial churches.

Stephen Williams, a Harvard graduate, was the first pastor. When he was ten, he was captured with his family by the Indians at the time of the Deerfield Massacre. He lived for a while with his captors. His sister, Eunice, stayed with the Indians and married one of them. Stephen was called the Indian Prince. He was one of those colorful New England scholars, well versed in the classics and in Biblical languages. He was given a settlement with which to build his house on the land granted him by the town with the understanding that he would spend his life as their teacher and counselor. He was a community builder, sharing the joys and sorrows of the parish, watching over the generations, a symbol to the people of stability and continuity, leading them in prayer and faith through crisis and change for sixty-seven years.

I often sat in my study in the church, writing at the simple pine table that had been his desk. I read there from his journal, kept with the discipline of the New England dominie, listing the failures and triumphs of faith. The former boy captive was associated with the scholars of New England and with the presidents of Dartmouth, Harvard and Yale. College presidents in those days were mostly Congregational ministers. I often wonder if they didn't do a better job training moral leaders than the promoters and fund raisers of today. In that era the football stadium was not considered the first priority of a college. There were no student riots and the faculty determined the curriculum.

Williams lived in his own home, serving his parish with a sense of permanence that modern ministers do not know. There were disputations and conflicts, but these New England pastors were fortresses of strength and their people held them in an esteem that helped preserve their peace of mind.

Longmeadow had its patriots and loyalists during the days of the Revolutionary War. Dr. Williams loved the mother country and the king and continued to pray for the royal family. At age eighty-two, he could not break the habit. In those days the congregation stood for prayer, the hinged pew seats turned up to provide more standing room. Certain parishioners expressed their protests against the pastor's royal leanings by slamming the seats and sitting down.

As the Revolution gained momentum, the patriarchal figure indicated deepening sympathy for the ideals of the Declaration of Independence. He wrote in his diary August 11, 1776: "Today I read publicly, being requested thereto by the Provincial Council, 'the Declaration of the Continental Congress for Independency.'"

When the War of 1812 ended, the townspeople rang the Paul Revere bell in the belfry until it cracked. It had to be taken to the famous bellmaker and revolutionist in Boston for repair.

Testimony of Nature

Behind Every Flower — A Story

When we took over the 1660 homestead there was a remnant of a perennial flower bed, a handful of survivors, in desperate need of the loving touch. We salvaged them from their anemic condition.

A stand of bee balm, *Monarda*, was true to its tradition of hardiness, being a native of the New World, an herb cherished for its medicinal qualities. The Indians made a potion from the leaves to treat chills. The pioneers used a similar mixture for skin irritations. The pink and red combs provided a welcome bouquet for a sick room, with the aromatic smell of the leaves and the fragrance of the bloom. Our specimens were pink lemon mint and a brilliant red known as Oswego tea. They both revived and extended themselves so we could split and move them and strengthen the ranks.

There was a clump of Shasta daisies, *Chrysanthemum Maximum*, in need of division and feeding. Their bright golden centers and white petals were dwarfed but still carried the proud tradition of open-faced cheer. These travelers from the Pyrenees mountains had crossed over to spread their brightness in the New World. John Bartram, a self-taught Quaker farmer who became

America's first noted botanist, was awakened to the call of nature by the sight of a daisy.

> One day (he wrote) I was very busy in holding my plow (for thee seeth I am but a plowman) and being weary I ran under the shade of a tree and reposed myself. I cast my eyes on a daisy. I plucked it mechanically and viewed it with more curiosity than common farmers are wont to do, and observed therein very many distinct parts. What a shame, said my mind, that thee shouldest have employed so many years in tilling the earth and destroying so many flowers and plants, without being acquainted with their structures and their uses!

He hired a man to finish the plowing, journeyed to Philadelphia where he bought a book in Latin by the botanist, Linnaeus. He engaged the schoolmaster to tutor him until he was able to understand the book. "Then I began to botanize all over my farm," he adds. He journeyed widely throughout the country until he had "knowledge of every tree and plant to be found in our continent."

We divided our daisy and coddled the two small plants. Today we still have a dozen offspring, compact flourishing bushes, three to four feet high, providing a profusion of blossoms three to four inches in diameter. Against this background of pure white innocence we have taken pictures of our children and grandchildren through the years, holding a daisy in a tiny fist.

One of our most romantic finds was a regal lily, *Lilium Regale,* which we nursed back to health. The life story of this gem is dramatic. Edmund H. Wilson brought the first bulbs from Tibet in 1910. He had heard reports of this fabulous flower while searching for plants in China for Kew Gardens. Later he was employed by Arnold Arboretum in Boston and was sent back to China to search for this lily which grew in a rocky valley among the snow-clad Himalayas of Tibet. He found it at the end of a long and arduous journey of many months. He recorded in his journal:

> There in narrow, semi-arid valleys, down which torrents thunder, and encompassed by mountains composed of mud shales and granite, whose peaks are clothed with snow eternal, the regal lily has her home. There in June, by the wayside, in rock-crevices by the torrent's edge and high up on the moun-

tainside and precipice, this lily in full bloom greets the weary wayfarer. Not in twos and threes, but in hundreds, in thousands, aye, in tens of thousands. Its slender stems, each from two to four feet tall, flexible and tense as steel, overtop the coarse grasses and scrub and are crowned with one to several large funnel-shaped flowers, each more or less wine colored without, pure white and lustrous on the face, clear canary yellow within the tube and each stamen filament clipped with a golden anther.

Wilson was injured by a landslide as he set out on his return from the border of Tibet to Szechwan. His leg was broken by the falling rocks. He was thrown across the narrow mountain trail. A mule caravan was following close behind. The path was not wide enough for them to turn back. They did not dare to stand still for fear of another rock slide. "There was only one thing to do. I lay across the path and the mules stepped over my body. There were nearer fifty than forty of them and each stepped clearly over me as if accustomed to such obstacles. Nevertheless, I breathed freely when the last one was over." His life was spared by the sure-footed mules.

He bound the leg with the wooden extensions of his camera tripod and his helpers carried him for many days to a missionary hospital. Infection had set in and amputation was considered, but the leg was saved by good fortune, notwithstanding months of delay and intense suffering. The natives wrapped the bulbs in clay and packed them in charcoal and mailed them to Boston. They were planted in the Arnold Arboretum where they flourished. We had one in our own garden. How long it had been there we cannot guess.

The only other plant worth salvaging was a delicate bleeding heart which proved to be a tenacious resident. *Dicentra* is an old-fashioned favorite with its fern-like leaves and graceful, drooping stems with their pendulous red, heart-shaped blossoms and a droplet at the point. It is a bold pioneer among the early bird perennials, unafraid of a sneak attack by Jack Frost. The intrepid Robert Fortune brought the plant from China, which he visited in 1843, studying the elaborate gardens of the Mandarins. I am grateful to him for this welcome floral announcer of Maytime, the bleeding heart.

The average person looking for a plant to purchase roams a nursery assuming that the charmer he finds has always been there, that it just evolved somehow. In reality, back of every flower is the story of a Bartram, a Linnaeus, a Wilson or a Fortune. Someone searched out the treasure in its native habitat. Someone patiently nurtured and improved it.

We should keep in mind, as we wander about in a profusion of the flowering handiworks of nature, that the assemblage reflects the dedication of horticulturists and botanists of many lands who have scoured mountains and valleys the world over to enrich our gardens.

The Miracle Called Spring

Sue and I had just returned to our Plymouth home, after a sojourn in tropical Florida, to witness the miracle of another New England spring. I opened the garage to be greeted by a barn swallow, flitting about the rafters, inspecting the mud nests that had been home for his ancestors. He was a lone scout sent ahead of his migrating kindred to check out the old apartments and see if they were in order. He saluted me in rapid, squeaky notes: *"eet wit, eet wit."* His glossy, blue-black plumage gave him dignity, enhanced by his ruddy throat and chest. True to family tradition, he returned to the spot where he was born.

Tipping his head, the scout looked down at me with twinkling black eyes, studying my car, still loaded with luggage, as if to say, "You make such a chore of going back and forth to the south with your car packed full of all kinds of things. You get lost on the Washington Belt Line and arrive weary. We travel light and return rested."

He seemed confident of a free rental for another season. It is a puzzle how he makes it back and how he gets in touch with his mate, who is somewhere south, waiting for the come on signal.

Does he plan to fly down after he has inspected the premises and meet her at some swallow motel along the Jersey Turnpike? Would they then make the last lap of the journey together to take over their nest of last summer or bring in mud from the brook and build a new one?

Before entering the house, we strolled about the premises on a tour of inspection and said, as we do each year, that there is no place like it. To observe the trees, shrubs and flowers on our Plymouth land in their awakening cycle every spring is an emotional experience. David Morton expresses this exultation in his poem "Expectancy":

> *Incredible! That in a day...an hour,*
> *Tomorrow...or the next day, it may be,*
> *The thing will happen here...A leaf or flower*
> *Will startle the young grass, and every tree*
> *Will wear a dim, grey softness, veiled and blurred,*
> *And there, a swift, blue darting of curved wings*
> *Will scarcely be believed in for a bird,*
> *So long and long expected — till it sings.*

The last days of April are golden hours — a thousand daffodils splashing color along our hedges and corners and unpruned forsythia cascading into feathery umbrellas. The Midas touch, which fits bright April, fades imperceptibly day by day. The daffodils and forsythia lose some of their gilded splendor. Slowly, with the blossoming of May, the landscape is transformed by new and deeper shades of green. The Norway maples sport their tufted circlets. Along the brook beyond the barn, yellow willow tendrils droop with the fantasy of a Chinese painting.

The fern leaf beech displays a coppery glow in its lacy unfoldings. The Japanese maple is a flaming magenta and the flowering crabs are blushing. Pink and yellow tulips sway gently. The warming sun from a cloudless sky pours over the stone wall. Bumblebees revel in the fragrant clusters of the Mayflower viburnum, intoxicated by this first nectar. A hazy, jade green tint hovers about the white dogwood, creating a soft, fairyland effect that embraces the earth. Bleeding heart, trillium, pulmonaria and candytuft are the first to blossom in the perennial bed, along with grape hyacinths and purple violets. Sea gulls dip and call overhead, scouting to see if any worms have been dug up in the garden. A song sparrow sings an aria from a budding white lilac near the toolshed.

No wonder the herring are running up the fresh water brook from the Atlantic, striving to reach the ponds where they can spawn. While fishing, I see them swirling and leaping, scorning my bait, intent on their pilgrimage. This annual spring migration from the sea comes at the same time the redwing blackbirds return. They are on hand to greet the silvery swimmers.

The lawns must be raked to make ready for their emerald rebirth, and the dandelion invasion faced. I scurry about on the earth like a chipmunk, with a sharpened digger in one hand, trailing a bushel basket that is soon brimming with golden discs and green leaves.

A catbird in the front hedge loosens his mimic tongue to improvise a few tuneful bars. He chooses to live near human dwellings where he can watch the household routine, playing hide-and-seek in the bushes, keeping a sharp eye on the environs, chatting and scolding, then bursting into song. A playboy, in gray swallowtail coat and black skull cap, he revels in splashing the bird bath and in guarding his territory.

Every morning brings a change of color, each day a fresh manifestation. Buttercups now speckle the orchard. Spring's creations are too priceless to endure. They are ephemeral, like moments of human happiness. I will match a New England seaside spring against every other entry — a grove of Florida's royal poinciana trees, a Carolina magnolia plantation, a Williamsburg formal garden, a Swiss Alpine midsummer village or a Devon thatched cottage surrounded by roses.

The prelude provided by the daffodils, forsythia and the greening earth is followed by apple blossom time. These trees produce their colonies of pink and white budlets warily, realizing that winter often sweeps back with blasts of cold when they grow over-confident. I have watched this orchard for forty-five seasons and have learned that the apples bloom May 10 to 12. And always, almost to the minute, I hear the mellifluous notes of the Baltimore orioles with flashes of orange and black in the midst of pink blossoms, the liquid euphony ringing out in the perfumed air. As punctual as a jumbo jet, they manage to return on schedule every year.

A pair are building their basket nest, laboring with string, yarn, thread, milkweed fiber and utilizing the shreds of cloth we hang on the lower branches. These birds mate for life. For years there has been a swinging nest in the elm. But, alas, the tree warden announced that Dutch elm disease had arrived. A noisome chain saw echoed sad tidings through the neighborhood as it decimated the old umbrella tree. When the birds flew back, they found that their home site had disappeared. Still trusting their instincts, they have set to work to rebuild in the maple that stands close to the house. They must be the same romantic couple. Some song birds live several years.

Now, once again, the golden sylphs flit about among the apple blossoms, darting like streaks of sunlight, warbling *"tu, teo, tee"* in bell-like cadence. This floral paradise seems to have been waiting for the coming of the oriole. He plays his role with gusto, summoning all creatures to join in a panegyric to the awakened earth.

The heyday of the orioles and apple blossoms fades in the midst of the much coming and going of other bird visitors. The flowering crabs are shedding their petals. The lilacs are now laden with royal clusters, a deeper hue than the wisteria on the kitchen ell. The perennial flowers produce the next act in their spring show with early poppies, Dutch iris and lilies of the valley.

The crescendo of flower, leaf and song does not, however, end with apple blossom time. Nature continues to produce another display with the genesis of the azaleas and rhododendron. A major exhibition of New England spring is provided by these vigorous evergreens with their massive clumps of blossoms in rapturous tints. These stellar performers stage an extravaganza, producing giant bunches with three or four clusters of orchid flowerets, as many as twenty to an assembly. They flaunt a riot of hues: cream, white, pink, rose, carmine, ruby, lavender and purple. This parade is accompanied by new faces in the perennial garden: peonies, coral bells, lupin, foxgloves, painted daisies and columbine.

Summer is another season, with its own offering yet to come.

As I studied this harbinger of summertime, I heard a mocking-bird singing from the ridgeboard of the house. He did a few runs and trills drawn from his storehouse, some tricks at mimicry, whistling like a cardinal and gurgling like a catbird. Then he lifted his head high and launched forth into creativity, producing his own unparallelled melody. It was an outpouring of dulcet tones, depth of feeling and perfection of delivery. This operatic star of the avian domain appeared to be saluting her majesty of flowerland, the rose.

The production captivated the chipmunk that stopped still on the stone wall, holding a violet leaf in his mouth. The robins halted their methodical exploration of the lawn to focus on the headliner above them. The bumptious wren ceased chirruping under the spell of the minstrel bard that offered his recessional to the vernal equinox. The mocker's overture to joy was a tribute to earth, sea and sky, a cadenza to the glory of the creator at the moment when summer said goodbye to spring and nature's drama moved on to another level of refulgence — to the first rose of summer.

We have had a rose garden for forty years. We are not expert or scientific gardeners. We just love flowers and grow them. We have adopted the motto of Linnaeus: "All for flowers." You will note that I have shifted from the singular to the plural. Not only would I be unable to nurture all our gardens with only two hands, but the pleasure would be so depleted that I am sure the flowers would soon show signs of malnutrition and neglect.

When Sue and I started life together, we felt that a garden was an essential part of our household menage. We have never been without one. Our present perennial bed is seventy-five feet long and fifteen feet wide, backed by a stone wall. Crawling on our kneepads, we are thrilled to uncover the delicate blue Alpine aster that has made its way through another season of cold and darkness to greet the warming sun, to pull a clump of witchgrass and see a madonna lily emerging for its twentieth spring. And there is the columbine peeping up and here is a purple delphinium we feared we had lost. Along the stone wall are signs of the faithful phlox that have performed bountifully for years.

We go on all fours through the length and breadth of this home of our floral friends, crawling in and out and around the plants and pulling the weeds up by their roots. All this bending, bowing and

creeping helps to moderate the natural arrogance of *Homo sapiens.*
I think this may prove wholesome for those of us who push our way
through life, ignoring the mystery and wonder of our world.

Now back to the roses. In April we move the marsh hay and
prune, using a freshly sharpened pruner. We wear gloves and long
pants because the thorns are sharp. We empty the compost pile onto
the rose bed and spade it in carefully, so as not to injure the roots,
along with some well-seasoned barn manure. We scatter a standard
rose food around the bushes. Then we start the watering schedule,
always in the morning so the leaves will dry by night.

The rose is a demanding lady, an all-consuming passion.
Enslaved by her beauty, we spend a lot of time and effort trying to
protect her against her chief foes, the Japanese beetles, black spot
and powdery mildew. We tie on our canvas pocket aprons every few
days and clip the dead heads and pick off all yellow and spotted
leaves.

By June fifteenth we are reveling in our roses, cutting and
preparing bouquets for our house, our church, the museums, the
hospital and our friends. Last year we cut a thousand blossoms and
left as many more on the bushes. We cut them half open to full
bloom, with some buds. We like a sort of cross section of the
generations. Each has its particular charm. There is a Chinese
proverb which says that flowers leave some of their fragrance in the
hand that bestows them. They certainly leave a gratifying feeling
with us, which is reward enough for our labors.

The thrill comes in arranging the variety of colors and fra-
grances. We take them to our kitchen sink and scrape off the thorns
from the stems with a keen bladed knife. This morning Sue brought
out of the cupboard a Victorian pedestal vase and in it she placed all
red roses, about two and half dozen, for the Antiquarian Museum.

She then chose a white ironstone bowl (from her grandmother's
bowl and pitcher set) and with the use of flower foam and tape
created a large, loose and flowing medley of breathtaking beauty
and set it on our hutch table in the keeping room. With a tablespoon
of chlorox and a little sugar added to the water, they should last for a
week. When they fade, we will save the petals for our daughter-in-
law, who makes potpourris for her garden club Christmas sale.

Friends ask us which is our favorite rose. Selecting a first among the queens is like trying to pick a star from the Milky Way. However, we will mention a few that we have grown successfully for many years: Garden Party, Christian d'Or, Pasquale, Fragrant Cloud, Sonia, Royal Highness, Appolo, Crimson Glory, Peace, Chicago Peace, King's Ransom, Kordis Perfecta, Oregold and Yankee Doodle. This last named rose is amazing in its holding quality. It has deep creamy buds that develop into globular blooms of sixty-five petals, flushed with pink, with one flower to a stem.

Some holy men pray before partaking of their morning meal. Before entering a mosque, the Moslems remove their shoes. We follow an equally sacred ritual. Before breakfast, or even a cup of tea, we walk barefoot over the dewy lawn to see what has opened in the rose garden overnight. And every evening we stroll through again, never failing to find some new revelation of beauty.

Sue says, "If I could choose my own ending, I should like, one early morning, to gather a huge armful of roses, while the dew is still on them, and sit down in that old cedar chair at the garden's edge, with the velvet petals touching my cheeks and their heavenly fragrance pervading the air — and just expire."

Keepers of the Garden

I understand why lily enthusiasts are captivated by these stately flowers with their spectacular range of colors and incomparable fragrance. They are symbols of purity and chastity. We decided to create a lily bed by the kitchen windows some time ago, not the most prestigious spot in our garden, but we could view our lilies at close hand throughout the day. Besides, we had a ready-made place where verbenas had flourished for years. But we were tired of clipping the faded blossoms. Of course, we have always grown a few lilies in the perennial garden, along with a variety of day lilies and old-fashioned Cape Codders. But we decided the *lilium* deserved an exclusive domain of her own. Like the rose, she is too regal to mingle with the motley miscellanea of flowerdom.

The land is slightly sloping, offering plenty of sun and a little shade, a situation favored by lilies. We removed the soil to a depth of eighteen inches, laid a base of gravel and sand for drainage, added some bone meal and cow manure, and replaced the loam we moved. We planted bulbs of short growing lilies in among the tall ones, since they like shade at their roots and flourish when their feet are cool (but not too wet) and their heads are warm. The resulting effect is one of a mass of blossoms from ground up. Lilies require little care. "They toil not, neither do they spin, yet Solomon in all his glory was not arrayed like one of these."

As I work among the lilies, feeding and mulching and securing them to bamboo stakes with twistems, I study the name tags at the base of each plant. They are, of course, in Latin, the universal language of flowers. This tradition does not irritate me since I studied Latin and also Greek, for which I am thankful, although today one can go through college and graduate school without ever tackling either, or any foreign language for that matter. I like traditionalism. It fits floriculture, adding dignity to these marvelous creations of nature.

Here in my little floral world, within reach of my outstretched arms, is a dazzling company: *Lilium Regale* (from China), with its pure white trumpet edged with delicate pink, a canary yellow throat, and each stamen clipped with a golden anther; *Lilium Pink Perfection*, lustrous in a dark pink with dusty zones; *Lilium Imperial Silver Strain*, pure white trumpets (ten inches in diameter) dotted with vermillion spots; *Lilium Speciosum* (from Japan), white speckled with rosy pink and crimson; *Lilium Firecracker*, upright vivid cherry scarlet bloom; *Lilium Golden Splendor*; *Ming Yellow*; *Speciosum Rubrum*; and *Lilium Zeus*; are just a few of our collection.

With their fallen pollen on my hands and their perfume rising like the alluring air of some blissful, magic island, I feel that I am, literally, in the Garden of Eden. The thought comes to me that gardening is a symbol of the harmonious relation between the human race and nature. According to the creation story in Judaism and Christianity, man's attitude toward the world is one of dominance and subjugation: "Be fruitful and multiply, and have dominion over the fish of the sea and over the birds of the air and over every living thing that moves on the earth."

In contrast, Islam draws a different lesson from the Garden of Eden. Mohammed taught that the Adam and Eve story represented God's plan "for man to dress the garden and keep it." His mission was not to rule the earth, but to create a paradise on earth. It looks as if Mohammed has been shortchanged.

For centuries, scholars of the Western world, who were friendly

with nature, who objected to the rigid Judaic and Christian tradition, have been condemned as heretics. Nature has long been considered to be carnal and pagan. In our era, naturalists and ecologists
are trying to turn the tables and look with favor on Mohammed's
concept that we are keepers, not lords of the garden.

The botanist who gave flowers their Latin names was the
pioneer, Carolus Linnaeus. He was the son of a Swedish Lutheran
minister. At the age of twenty-five, he made his famous peregrina-
tion, alone and on foot, to Lapland, searching the unexplored
country for plants and flowers. He endured privation and danger in
order to add to the human knowledge of nature, seeking to protect
the work of the creator. Like Mohammed, he considered himself a
keeper of the magnificent garden that a master designer had brought
into being for the use and enjoyment of man. Following years of
intimate association with the flowers of the globe, Linnaeus wrote
his "Credo of a Botanist," eloquent as a Hebrew psalm:

If, therefore, the Maker of all things, who had done
nothing without design, had furnished this earthly globe, like
a museum, with the most admirable proof of his wisdom and
power; if, moreover, this splendid theater would be adorned in
vain without a spectator; and if he placed in it Man, the chief
and most perfect of all his works, that he may observe in them
the evident marks of divine wisdom:

Thus we learn not only from the opinions of moralists
and divines, but also from the testimony of nature herself, that
this world is destined to the celebration of the Creator's glory,
and that man is placed in it to be the publisher and interpreter
of the wisdom of God; and indeed he who does not make
himself acquainted with God from the consideration of nature,
would scarcely acquire knowledge of him from any other
source; for 'If we have no faith in things which are seen, how
should we believe those things which are not seen?'

I admire Linnaeus the achiever, his insights into how our
world operates, the enjoyment he found in nature and the philosophy of life that he developed. I wish I could have known him.

A Flash of Color and a Song

Music in the Air

Many years ago in China, I admired the custom of presenting birds as gifts and the tradition of walking with one's bird, carrying it on a hand perch or in its cage. Then, birds of shopkeepers were hung in front of stores on mild days so that one heard bird songs along busy streets. There was a gatekeeper at the old Manchu compound, where we lived in Peking, who cherished his petite brown and yellow lark. At night he kept it carefully covered with a blue cloth hood while it was cool, lifting it off when the sun was shining.

This kindly little man in a clean cotton robe and black skull cap cared for the bird tenderly, making sure that it was fed first, before he fried his flour cakes and poured his tea. He talked to it and slept with the cage close beside him. And when the weather was warm, he hung the cage and the lark under the eaves of his gate-house, where the bird would sing for him while he enjoyed a smoke, sitting on a wooden bench with his long-stemmed pipe, keeping an eye on the gate. The lark was the joy of his life.

So, too, have been the pleasures of my life with birds, although I have preferred to observe them free in their habitats. I need not go beyond my own yard to find the pleasure of their company. Within twenty feet of my back door, a pair of woodpeckers are nesting and flying in and out among the branches of the maple tree. They cluck to each other as they scurry up and down and forage about, murmuring *"chew, chew, chew."* Pert and aggressive, they go about their assignment of policing the bark with sharp eyes alert for bugs and beetles.

Two small, pinkish-brown doves are nesting in the lilacs. Being ground feeders, they are seen on the lawns and in the fence rows of the neighborhood. I note how close they keep to each other and how they coo, expressing their devotion during mating time. It is not difficult to feel that they are capable of affection akin to human love. The larger mourning doves, dressed in the same soft, roseate frocks, spend most of their time on top of buildings and telephone wires, where they study the area. They call in a low-pitched, slow tempo, with a touch of contentment and melancholy intermixed.

Robins, too, are building in the dense fothergilla bush by the kitchen door. They like to be close to human dwellings. Earlier in the season, a wind storm destroyed their nest in the dogwood tree and three azure blue eggs, but they are trying again nearby.

Through some happy circumstance, the cardinal began to visit us in recent years, adding his dashing red coat and his bell-like whistle, *"what-cheer, what-cheer"* to my corner of New England. Some of his company enjoyed our Yankee terrain and menu so well that they even wintered with us. They were welcomed to our feeders and offered such delicacies as hot roasted peanuts, peanut butter and deluxe sunflower seed. This Don Juan makes a devoted father, watching over his mate, carrying food to her while she nests and taking care of their young. I see them in the hedge feeding on insects, seed and wild fruit.

The red bird may have engaged in a bit of sales promotion in the southland and told the mocking birds about the bounteous display of flowers, berries, bugs and worms that we have to offer up here. The mockers were enticed to make the migratory flight from their land of magnolias and jasmine to inspect our apple blossoms and blueberries, to sip cooling drinks from our brooks and lakes. These artists in ashy gray were soon captivating us with their performances from roofs and treetops.

This bird boasts no brilliant dress, but he is handsome and intelligent. He is a glamorous actor in the opera staged by nature, the Orpheus of birddom. He carries his music wherever he goes, warbling from a tree, telephone wires or a lamp post. I heard two singers waging a contest in a Plymouth shopping center, where a new building was being erected. The sound of the cement mixer and the electric saw seemed to challenge them to transform disharmony into melody.

Often caught up in his own exuberance, the singer moves his tail and wings in time as he trips about like a ballet dancer. The whistle of a cardinal may set him off in a series of improvisations as he mimics his neighbor's calls. After warming up his sound equipment with these playful exercises, he will launch into higher levels of creativity, demonstrating his skill as the master singer, spreading *joie de vivre* abroad.

The mocker likes people and enjoys performing for them. A playful buffoon, he teases the dog or the cat. With such artistry, one would expect him to be a snob, but he is chummy and informal. He sings day or night and is at his best when the moon is full.

Sometimes, while I am writing on the terrace, he flies on top of the rhododendron nearby. Conscious of the clatter of my typewriter, he casts an eye in my direction. I turn on a portable radio, fortunately finding an orchestral air that catches the ear of the musician. He responds by tuning up, bursting with happiness at the discovery of this unexpected accompaniment and sets out with vigor to produce a musical for my benefit and continues with gracious abandon until his mate appears. She twitters appreciation of his talent, nudges close to him and they fly off to their nest.

Last October thirtieth, I heard one bold, late mocker repeating a midsummer recital. I had never heard anything like it on the bird network staged in this frosty New England setting. Although they are little creatures of nature, birds win human admiration because of the beauty of their plumage and the glory of their songs and also, I think, because of their remarkable, mysterious powers. Their notes are repeated year after year, each species preserving its score. How, I wonder, do they learn their widely varied melodies and what keeps their lyrics alive through the centuries?

Major-domo of the Garden

I ease into the rose garden, with a watchful eye on the bees that are pillaging the fragrant petals. The wrens are at their posts, atilt on the rail fence. The two brown mites gurgle with zest as they carry out their daily inspection of the premises: *"De, de de de."* They are always on hand when I walk into the yard, chattering to each other as if they carried walkie-talkies. This intercommunication between male and female is handy, since they live in a bushy environment.

Ever on the move, they shoot from fence to shrub, from shrub to tree, like miniature rockets. Rain or shine, they greet each day with exuberance, dashing about with zestful spirit, twittering cheerfully. Although a crude architect and a casual builder, the wren contributes camaraderie to his neighborhood. The pert cock builds several nests which he shows his mate. She picks one and he keeps a spare to use as a retreat when the house is crowded with demanding offspring or he craves peace from his scolding spouse. These dwellings are furnished with rubble he collects.

This spring I noted a cock carrying twigs to an old bird house in the Chinese kousa back of the perennial bed. The next day I placed a new box house in the pink dogwood by the rail fence of the rose garden. Bright eyes spotted it and he immediately busied himself carrying little branches, trying to push them through the small, round entrance. His mate approved his choice. They moved in and have passed the summer days raising their broods in the new dwelling.

In spite of his mediocre reputation as an architect, the wren has been a favorite in legend. According to the European fable, he was chosen as monarch of the air. During a dispute as to which bird should be their leader, it was decided to stage a contest and determine which could fly the highest. The contenders took off and flew skyward. The eagle, with a powerful wingspread, rose above all of them. As it prepared to announce that it was at the highest point, a wren slipped from the eagle's back, where it had hidden itself, and winging its way above the mighty creature, broadcast the news that it was to be their king.

This folk tale caught the fancy of humans who admired the spirit of this debonair sprite and awarded him the title. The gesture was a recognition of a small member of the animal kingdom whose lithesome spirit triumphed over power and size.

Etiquette in Birddom

The lovemaking of birds creates a joyous hubbub in our yard, meadow and orchard every spring. Our place is alive with solicitous couples entranced by the ritual of courtship. I can identify them by their plumage and their song: robin, song sparrow, oriole, wren, catbird, cardinal. They sweep out in pursuit of each other, cheeping messages, billing and cooing, warbling melodies and building nests. They are caught up in the etiquette of mating time and the air is full of excitement and promise.

I was reading the other day about the jackdaws, those plain lookers who can boast no gay apparel but who are romanticists. I recall seeing them at the majestic Wells Cathedral in South England. That summer I watched them constructing their nests on the buttresses and window ledges of the cathedral.

I rested on a bench in the solitude of the close, studying these clever birds that often choose churches for their dwelling place. I admire their taste and their courtship and marriage practices. They fall in love and are betrothed for a year before they enter their lifelong partnership. The male is a devoted partner, calling out 'zich, zich, zich'' from the nesting site he chooses, inviting his fiancé to join him. The young couple stay close together, proud of their love, defending each other, engaging in expressions of tenderness. The female caresses the neck feathers of the male and he closes his eyes in blissful delight.

This encounter started my research on courtship etiquette in the bird world. When that mating call sounds, the males groom their plumage and go forth to seek some charmer of their own heritage that eats the same bugs or seeds and upholds the customs of the clan. Birds of paradise spread feathery plumes and sound soft bugle notes. The trumpeter swans, that marry for life, perform water ceremonies and stage their own swan lake ballets. Grebes, which boast silken plumage and feathery horns, also engage in an extravaganza of water dancing.

I observe feathered friends every season reaffirming their faith in romance. I admire their touch of the amorous in the daily round. They not only vocalize at mating time, but feed spouse and chicks and tend to family chores. I am impressed by the courtship practices of the penguins that show off like diminutive clowns, bowing and bobbing. They bounce about with vigor, maintaining the ritual of their ancestors in a hostile world of rocks, snow and ice. These jaunty partners share the nest in shifts, sitting out the howling blizzards on their frigid hatcheries, fasting for weeks to raise their brood, performing their genuflections like well mannered Japanese.

I have come to the conclusion, in my observations of birds, that a goodly number of males shape up to the standards of the Equal Rights Movement and have fairly clean records when it comes to male chauvinism. They are gallant suitors, competent house builders, attentive to their spouses. They provide groceries for their offspring and defend the family in time of danger.

The formalities practiced by my avian friends add spice and color to spring and summer. They enliven the daylight hours with the display of their plumage, exhibiting deference to mates and showing courtesy and mutual admiration. They produce bars of music to lighten my hours with lawnmower, shovel, hoe and pruner.

I am saddened as mating time ebbs and the birds begin to ease up in the care and feeding of their children, moderate the exuberance of their singing and move in a slower tempo. As summer wanes, they grow more introspective, possibly anticipating their exodus and wondering how their fledglings will measure up on the impending journey. In keeping with the shrinking hours of daylight, they soften the outbursts of song which have cheered my daily rounds. They twitter and talk. Then one day there is a sudden void and I know they have disappeared in the blue vault above.

Gossamer Wings

This morning I was cutting off the withered heads of some late blooming Shasta daisies, when I spotted a monarch butterfly resting on a clump of white phlox. Its wings of orange brown bore intricate black and white markings as if designed by an abstract painter. They were worthy to adorn a piece of jewelry. I squinted closely at the silken wings fluttering on the snowy blossoms. They were storing up nectar to build strength for their incredible journey south. And at the close of the perilous excursion, after respite in the sunshine, this fragile ornament, with gossamer wings, would be stirred by the urge to start back to the barren pastures of New England.

I am continually amazed at the loyalty of nature's children. This happens to be a milkweek butterfly. That explains a lot. Its ancestral eggs were deposited on a milkweed plant in some wind-blown field in this north country. The caterpillar that evolves feeds on the poisonous plant which is shunned by cattle, horses and sheep. It is estimated that monarch caterpillars devour tons of this nuisance weed every season. This heartens the farmers who wage a losing battle against the intruder.

In my own meadow I fight the tenacious milkweed which has been romanticized by poets who write of its golden pods releasing silken messengers that drift dreamily about, seeking a strategic spot to take root. Season after season I knock them down with my sickle or sweep them away with the swish of my scythe. Their pithy stalks ooze a milky fluid when attacked, but their wounds heal quickly to produce their pod harvest. Each seed packet is a work of imaginative form.

I see milkweed in scores of old pasture lands throughout New England, scorned by the livestock as well as by the farmer. It is somehow reassuring that nature has found one use for the odious weed. It is the delivery room and nursery for the monarch butterfly. And in deference to the agriculturists, the butterflies agree to devour as many plants as possible.

The milkweed rewards the monarchs that emerge from the chrysalis, rendering them undesirable and lethal to beasts and birds that would eat them if they were not inheritors of the milkweed's poison. So the weed helps the butterflies and the butterflies help the farmer. During the summer, they break forth from their chrysalis darkness in this miracle of transformation and begin to explore their aerial world. It moves me to think that this may have taken place in my own field close to the blueberry patch where the indestructible plant grows.

The graceful flyers soon become conscious of their obligation to mate and propagate their heritage. Eggs are deposited with their ancestral host. With the shortening days of autumn, the many splendored wings are seized by a compulsion to turn south. Multitudes of them congregate, swarms that grow into incredible clouds of brilliant color. Aided by unknown forces, this massive movement of neophyte flyers follows the path of migrating birds down the seacoast to the warmth that can save them from wintry death. Some are blown over the ocean and perish, others fall by the way from storm, hunger and fatigue.

It is estimated that some of them log 4,000 miles during their brief life span. Millions of them set forth for Mexico. At some rest stations they cling together on trees in such density that their orange and brown wings cover the leaves and camouflage them. Eventually the fortunate reach their sanctuary and bask in tropical bliss. Some will live to return to springtime fields of the northland and so keep alive the incomparable monarch tradition.

The entomologist, George Ordish, published in his book, *The Year of the Butterfly*, the thrilling record of the journey of two monarchs. Pliable, the female, emerged as an adult butterfly September 12 in Glen Falls, New York. She was tagged and set out on her journey south. Timorous, the male, was tagged September 16 and released. They took different routes, flying over New York, New Jersey, Virginia, the Carolinas and Texas to Lake Champayan, Mexico. Timorous arrived December 4, covering 2,000 miles in the seventy-nine days. Pliable came along fourteen days later. They traveled by the sun, following railroad tracks, rivers and their native instincts, surviving winds, rain and many perils.

The Mexican paradise welcomed them with sunshine and fragrant flowers.This lovely spot was alive with monarchs that had made the pilgrimage. Timorous was looking for a mate. He found Pliable. A Mexican naturalist observed them courting and mating and reported his findings to Glen Falls, New York.

March 18 Pliable felt the compulsion to start north. She made a number of stops on her course to lay eggs on milkweed plants, searching for and choosing healthy leaves that would nourish her offspring. On the last lap of her journey, her wings tattered, she fell exhausted on the ground in Stevenson, Maryland. Ants attacked her and she expired. On May 1 her wings were found and her label number reported.

Timorous was caught in a storm off Myrtle Beach, South Carolina and swept out to sea. The flights of these two ended tragically, but they had fulfilled their mission by mating and depositing their eggs along the route; and their children, emerging from their chrysalis stage a few weeks later, followed them on the flight to the northland.

I ask myself how this mite of a being can cope with an arduous life cycle, beginning in the form of a caterpillar that weighs a thousandth of an ounce. Even the adult butterfly is frail as translucent tissue, a fairy creation. By contrast, a newborn blue whale weighs a ton. Yet nature has plans for great and small, each one contributing to the sum total.

The Marvel of Avian Migrations

The Manomet Bird Observatory is about a mile from my house on Manomet Point, a high promontory that looks out over the broad Atlantic. It is an ideal spot in which to study birds. The area is dense with trees and underbrush, including pitch pine, black oak and Japanese walnut. What makes it especially appealing to birds is that berry shrubs such as black cherry, shad bush, arrowwood, blueberries and wild honeysuckle, which abound, furnish food. The location is a perfect touch-down and take-off point for all manner of land and sea birds.

Yesterday I had nothing special on the docket, so I took a hike over to the observatory. It was a clear day with wispy, cirrus clouds and a touch of fall in the air, ideal for walking. I wanted to watch some bird banding.

A student intern guided me down a hillside toward the sea. I saw nets stretched among the windblown thickets and scrub pine. They were about eight feet high, a light weight, and not so fine a mesh as the ones we use to catch minnows. We walked about fifty feet when I spied a tiny brown bird caught in the netting. It fluttered when the student disentangled it and took it in his hands.

"A song sparrow," he said, "about a year old." He placed it in a cloth bag, carried it inside the laboratory, weighed it, and clamped a light aluminum tag on one of its tan colored legs. He spoke gently to the trembling captive, set it free and it soared up and away. He entered a record in his notebook and we passed outside along the wall of netting.

The next capture was a downy woodpecker that appeared distraught over his predicament, but soon recovered poise in the friendly hands of the young naturalist, registering a chirp of protest over his captivity.

Then came a cardinal, a rare beauty in that drab net, a striking example of the splendor of the bird kingdom, a flashing knight in brilliant red costume. I couldn't resist touching the silken plumage of his crested head. He jerked away from me proudly. After all, he was one of the royalty of birddom. He took off after his brief physical.

A red knot, caught and banded here, was later recovered in Victoria, Brazil, having traveled 4,200 miles. Brian Harrington, shorebird biologist at the observatory, is an authority on the migrations of the North American red knot. He considers them the champion long distance flyers. They surpass the arctic terns that execute a similar round trip but cannot equal the red knot for non-stop travel. They log about fifty miles an hour. I asked him how far they could fly without coming down to feed. He speculated that they might make the journey non stop from the James Bay in Hudson Bay to the northeast corner of South America.

The knots nest in the arctic Hudson Bay area and winter in southern Argentina. The bulk of the population, estimated at 200,000, stops in Surinam and Guyana before settling down on the coast between Chubuta and Tierra del Fuego. A small group have chosen southwest Florida for their winter home. These chunky little birds, with salmon colored breasts and speckled brown head and plumage, are about nine inches from bill to tail. They weigh around 120 grams at the end of the journey. After hearty feeding, they will reach as much as 200 grams. They complete their round trip of 20,000 to 24,000 miles each year. Their life span is five to six years. Some may live for ten years.

The observatory has banded over 5,000 knots. Many are also

color marked. They have been picked up in Florida, the Caribbean, Central America and South America. The May 1983 *Audubon Magazine* carried a picture of Harrington taken in Argentina holding a red knot that he had banded in Plymouth. He was smiling with pleasure at this thrilling experience.

The Manomet Bird Observatory has set up observation posts on the coast of the Western Hemisphere with thirty-five nations cooperating. Volunteer observers report all knots they can identify during the migration season with special attention to banded and color dyed birds.

The red knots use our Plymouth and Scituate beaches as a stop over on their way from Hudson Bay to Southern Argentina. They have flown over my house for countless years and some have wintered near my place in Florida. They visit us in mid August on their journey south and again on their return in May.

These remarkable birds manage to show up when the lunch counters along the way are spread for them. They return to the same feeding grounds. In Florida they eat coquina clams and in Delaware Bay they enjoy a banquet of crab eggs. This timely visit coincides with the full moon egg laying of the horseshoe crabs in May. In Plymouth and Scituate they feast on mussels, small crustaceans and worms from the salt water flats, much the same diet they enjoyed in Argentina. Then they leave us for the last lap of their journey, arriving in the arctic to start nesting on the snow-covered earth.

This is only one of the believe-it-or-not records that emerge from the research of these dedicated naturalists. Looking out from Manomet Point, which has been in the migratory path of birds for centuries, I think of the wonder of avian wings. The phalarope nests in pot holes on the Great Plains and winters on lakes in the Andes. The white storks breed on rooftops in Germany, returning in early fall to South Africa. Whooping cranes raise their young on the edge of the Arctic Circle and winter on the the Gulf Coast of Texas.

I wonder who gives directions for these long distance tours? Who says: "You chaps go to South Africa; you fellows can have the Texas Coast; and you head for the Andes Mountains"?

As I stood under the fall sky, I sensed that the hegira was under way. The colorful companions of summer were gathering and departing. No longer do the chummy swallows greet me from the rafters of the garage. I miss their aerial maneuvers at twilight. The convivial wrens have deserted their posts on the rail fence. The jeweled helicopter of the flower garden, the hummingbird, is enroute to the tropics.

How do they know when to fly south and when to return north? How do they organize and make ready? How do they set their course and know when to rest, where to find food, how to deal with rain, wind and fog? They must use extraordinary senses and operate by the sun and the stars and the internal clock they seem to possess. In their navigation they may employ the earth's magnetic field and possibly its gravitational field. Eighteen laysan albatrosses were shipped from Midway Island to the Marshall Islands and the Philippines, some 4,200 miles away. When released, fourteen of these flyers made it back safely to their Midway homes.

When I think of the cruise of that sea bird, the red knot, and the pole to pole round trip of the arctic tern, I am confounded with wonder. Avian wings become symbols to me of the human mind and its capacity to explore earth, sea and sky. They fill me with awe for the order that prevails about me and the organisms, small and great, that live in accord with its interlocking structure.

Friendly Voices of the Night

A city dweller might feel lonely here on our quiet country road when all night long the only car that passes is the comforting police cruiser on its customary rounds. There are no night clubs, no theater, none of the gaiety and excitement of the metropolis. It might seem boring to listen to such modest communicators as song sparrows, katydids and Canada geese. But as the days pass and one sinks into a state of relaxation, the voices of nature speak more clearly in their gentle ways and the habit of living with sunrise and sunset and with the ebb and flow of tides begins to pay dividends in repose and contentment.

It is pleasant to hear the call of a bird, the chirp of an insect, to reach out in a new dimension of silence. At eventide a calm enfolds the place. The sounds of the day are muted. The countryside rests in a mood of reverie. "Reverie, like the rain of night, restores color and force to thoughts which have been blanched and wearied by the heat of the day," wrote Henry Amiel.

In the springtime I listen to the peepers welcoming the darkness, to the keening of the gulls in a shadowy sky and to the haunting sweetness of the song sparrow's subdued goodnight.

In summer the green-coated katydid chooses twilight to rub the file on the scraper of his wing, performing from the tree where he has passed the daylight hours in silence. Now he reminds earth of the coming of night.

Brown thrashers often introduce their talents to help create the mystery of nightfall. They usually call from the jungle of brush along the brook but now and then one will fly close to the house and sing from the lilac hedge, which affords him protection as he silently swoops about.

One evening this summer a full moon floated above the tree line along the shore, luminous and hypnotic. A mocking bird from the oak woods across the road, charmed by the gentle intrusion of golden light, produced a lullaby for his mate that lingered in the air like an antiphon. I felt with the poet, Richard Burton, that words would profane the glory of the moment:

> *Thy beauty haunts me heart and soul,*
> *O thou fair moon, so close and bright.*
> *Though there are birds that sing this night*
> *With thy white beams across their throats,*
> *Let my deep silence speak for me*
> *More than for them their sweetest notes.*

My ears have become more sensitive to the night sounds of the country. I have learned to listen to the soporific rhythm of the fog horn at the Gurnet Light, to the resounding waves on the beach, the cradling wind in the maple and the pitter-patter of raindrops on the roof.

The cricket comes to my hearth in early fall, during the closing hours of the day, with his cheery *creeket, creeket.* He creeps out of his spot in the old floor board which had furnished a home for wood worms and other beetles before he arrived. Happy in the drab environment, rich with the odor of antiquity, he hops to the fireplace hearth, which provides a pulpit for him to express himself.

His chirping is the only sound in the stillness. He offers his companionship to the household as darkness comes on. I understand why the Chinese and Japanese like the crickets, build elaborate cages for them and treat them as pets. Jean Henri Fabre said, "I know of no insect voice more gracious, more limpid in the profound peace of the nights of August." When I hear the little creature chirping, I feel the cozy embrace of home.

Urban existence robs one of the autumn encounter with wild geese, but I watch them every fall. I saw a flock the other evening, winging their way over my house in V formation. They honked down to me in a friendly goodbye. I held their orderly departure to faraway southern waters in view until they faded out of sight.

The stars and the firmament are brighter here over my corner of New England with its unpolluted air. The heavenly bodies speak more clearly to me from the wide sweep of infinity. Here in this seaside setting, I have grown closer to nature.

I often think of Thomas Carlyle's words about the nurture that silence offers us:

> Silence, the great empire of silence! Silence and the great silent men! Scattered here and there, each in his own department, silently thinking, silently working; whom no morning newspaper makes mention of. They are the salt of the earth. A country that has none or few of these is in a bad way. Like a forest which has no roots, which has all turned to leaves and boughs; which must soon wither and be no forest at all.

Quiet grows more pervasive with the coming of winter, when insect calls and bird songs disappear. Bare trees dominate the open landscape. The ocean seems closer at hand and the breakers more audible. Gulls and owls remain with the feeder visitors, the chickadees, juncos and woodpeckers that twitter with subdued voices, never rivaling their colorful cousins of summer that bubble with music. Fields and woodlands are somber, passing their sleeping time under leafless branches above the frozen, brown earth. While dark clouds scuttle overhead, earth waits to see what the next move of nature will bring. There is an expectant stillness with the falling snow.

I can understand why Sir Walter Raleigh met the strife of the Elizabethan Age with the request: "Give me my scallop shell of quiet."

When the Whippoorwills Call

Last night we took our evening turn about the garden. The yard was sweet with the fragrance of nicotiana. The moon spotlighted the gold leaf horse on the barn. My forebears have looked up at this weathervane for generations. The golden legs are spread as in a canter and the head is held high. The whippoorwills were responding to the spell of the night. The gentle, mottled gray, brown and buff birds, with a white band across their throats and black whiskers beside their bills, are hermits. They live secluded lives, hidden away in lowly nesting places, flitting noiselessly about, feeding on nocturnal bugs. These mobile insect traps are a boon to man.

They sounded their romantic notes from the thickets below the barn. They have flown in from the Gulf of Mexico to nest along the stream loved by their ancestors. They make their migratory journey by night, guided by discerning eyes. In their nighttime hunting, they fly low, sailing around shrubs and bushes, twisting and turning in pursuit of their food. They methodically chant their three notes in a rhythmic spell: *"whit-er-wee, whit-er-wee, whit-er-wee."*

Responding to the voices from the brook, another woodland

dweller, who lives in monastic seclusion, the recluse thrush, flung out his melody like a bell: *"Oo-oo-aylila, aylila, aylila."* This songster lifted the summer vespers to a new level. The reddish-brown singer was rendering the melodious nocturne that his predecessors have preserved through the centuries.

I thought of the generations of my family who lived here. They stand behind me, as it were, so that I cannot see them clearly. I hear only echoes of their words, scattered phrases of the messages they left behind. But I feel the influence of their lives touching me in very definite ways.

Inheritance is a powerful force. I see both my paternal and maternal grandfathers in myself. From one I inherited my tall, slender stature, my brisk manner of walking, my excellent digestive system and my short toenails. (He was a doctor of medicine.) From my paternal side I received my heavy shock of prematurely gray hair, my affinity with nature and my naiveté in the monetary world. (He was a doctor of divinity.)

Too many of the present generation seem caught up in a supercilious disregard of their forefathers. They make light of their relations with the past and speak condescendingly of tradition. We are oversold on the "generation gap" which severs us from family ties and the accumulated wisdom of those who lived before us, which is a sad waste of knowledge.

A panorama of ten thousand summer nights hovered over brook, orchard and meadow. A vista from the past haunted the farmhouse, recalling far-off yesterdays. Now, as then, the herring stage their upstream marathon, birds mate in the tangle of wild roses along the stream and the stars keep their steadfast watch. There is promise for the future of the whippoorwill and thrush and the dwellers in the old house.

The Blessed Earth

The Blessed Earth

Every human wants to own a piece of earth. My small acreage is more than the square footage on the assessor's map. It could produce food for a cow and chickens and enough vegetables and fruit for me as long as I live. I own what is inside the ground as deep as I can dig. If there is oil or gold down there, it is mine. Land is the soundest investment in the world.

Captain Knowles, our neighbor, a weatherbeaten master of his own sailing ships, was ninety-two years old when he placed his seven-room Victorian house and four acres on the market in 1937. His wife had died and he was planning to live with his son. He asked four thousand dollars. Someone offered him two thousand. He tapped his cane sharply on our brick terrace, vowing he would not give it away. He would leave it to his son instead. "I have sailed this globe around and there is just so much earth on it and it can never be increased!" he said. The captain was right. Today his place is worth twenty times his asking price.

I have watched children playing on beaches all over the world. They are caught up in euphoria as they grab handfuls of sand and let it sift through their fingers. They repeat this over and over, infatuated by their affinity with the earth. And making mud pies is a universal joy of childhood.

People in all lands love the soil. I recall a scene in North China in the spring of the year, when on a visit to the country. A farmer was plowing on the plain, following a black ox, tugging at the wood shaft of his primitive plow, turning the brown soil in neat furrows, guided by the skill of his forefathers who had tilled this land for generations. These lonely figures against the range of hills might have stepped from the canvas of a T'ang artist.

A cloud of dust eddied about them in the barren, rust-colored landscape. Their labor indicated that all man cherished came from the ground below and around him. The houses he built, the beds that offered him repose, the food that fired his lagging energy, the clothes he wore, the jade and silver he admired, all came from the dark and aged mystery.

Alas, Mao Zedong took over the farmer's land and he was moved to one small room in the cement barracks of the commune where he could be constantly enlightened by self-criticism and struggle meetings. I am sure, now and then, he steals away from the radio and sits alone, looking out to the Western Hills, dreaming of his mud-brick cottage and plot of land, his small piece of the blessed earth.

I thank God that in America we still hold title to our land. In earlier years our neighbor, Octavius Reamy, came with his black horse and hand plow to turn over our garden plot that had been planted off and on for about three centuries. I loved to be present on those late April days, when the soil was ready for plowing, to watch the corn stubble and the bedraggled remnants of last summer's garden disappear under the sandy brown soil.

Eager to begin the first planting, I stood there laying out in my mind a plan for the peas which would be the first seed dropped into the shallow trench made by my hoe under the line stretched between fresh-cut willow sticks. Then would follow other hardy faithfuls like lettuce, radishes, beets and chard; and the springtime ritual would be underway. I was caught up in the dream of the gardener who plants with high anticipation, trusting that sun and showers will share a blissful partnership with him, that the birds will be kind and spare the seed and that this will be a summer free from bugs and blight.

One for the Blackbird

Every spring when I plant corn, I think of Squanto who introduced the vegetable to the Pilgrims. He showed them how to plant five grains to a hill, with three herring for fertilizer, their heads turn in, their tails turned out, covering them carefully with soil so that wolves would not dig up the fish and the crows would not eat the corn. He said to plant when the leaves on the oak trees were the size of a squirrel's ear. Wise Squanto picked the oak, the last tree to leaf, thus coping with those fickle New England springs that can nip the tender blades of corn.

While planting, I chant the old blessing: "One for the blackbird, one for the crow, one for the cut worm and two to grow."

As Squanto well knew, the alewives innocently offered themselves to the maize planters by staging their pilgrimage to the ponds just in time to be scooped up and used as fertilizer. I am too tender-hearted to ask them to make that sacrifice. Besides, I think cow manure is just as effective and if not available, I turn to an application of 5-10-5 from the bag in the barn.

This English-speaking Indian not only acted as the Pilgrim's interpreter with the Wampanoags but also as their guide to appreciation of nature in the New World. He taught them how to fish, dig clams, hunt turkeys and deer, where to find edible greens, fruits and nuts. He explained the role of maize in his culture, a basic food unknown to the English. He introduced the newcomers to the flora and fauna of New England.

The Pilgrims lived in a natural world, free from the complications of congestion and pollution, from the controls of royal families and the ecclesiastical hierarchy. They were forced to draw on their own resources from local surroundings. I have concluded that they survived by their faith in God and by strength they drew from nature.

William Bradford and Edward Winslow, the chief early chroniclers, paid tribute to the majesty of God's creation. They knew the power of the sea. Much of their food came from its depths. They studied the tides and planned their labor around them and found strength in nature's constancy.

They must have developed a sense of smell far more delicate than twentieth century people because there was nothing to dilute the fragrance of the pines, grasses and flowers, the aroma of oak fires on their hearths and the tang of the ocean air. Walking along the trails through the woods, they reveled in the virgin forest, uncontaminated by dumps, sewage, smokestacks and chemical waste. There were no highway signs, no neon lights, no thundering cavalcades of motors belching noxious fumes. A traveler could enjoy birds warbling in the trees, pines soughing in the breeze and flowers nodding pleasant greetings. Our forefathers were grateful for the bounty of fresh-flowing, pure spring water from which visitors may still refresh themselves today.

The first spring, when they saw the buds opening on the maples, heard the song sparrows calling and washed their clothes in the soft water of Town Brook, spreading them on the green grass to dry, they must have felt strength welling up in their veins. They literally breathed in nature's vitality in the smell of the new cut shingles and thatch, fresh from the pond. Pottery mugs of trailing arbutus filled their cottages with fragrance.

These settlers worked with nature, planting the seed they had carried in small packets from England, guarding the wheat, barley, rye, peas and beans through the first winter, protecting them from rats and mice, from wet and mold. They planted them with a prayer and with the ingathering of the first meager harvest, they planned a time for Thanksgiving and invited their Indian neighbors to share in tribute to nature and her divine Creator.

Edward Winslow recorded: "Our harvest being gathered in, our Governor sent four men a'fowling, that some might, after a more special manner rejoice together, after we had gathered the fruit of our labors."

There was pleasure in their out-of-door life, working in the fields, in the woodlands, at the grist mill, hunting in the meadows for partridge and quail and in the marshes for ducks and geese.

I like roast duck and goose and often think of the happy hunting grounds of the Pilgrims. Some time ago I joined a duck shooting expedition on Cape Cod. We carried a battery of high-priced guns. We wore red caps and approved hunting jackets. It was ten above zero (about par for good ducking). We took refuge in a scientifically designed blind, bundled up, with our thermos bottles full of hot coffee. The sky was a somber gray with heavy snow flakes falling. "Ideal for ducks," our mentor advised.

We stuck it out for several hours, sighting only three ducks. We managed to bag one. Our coffee being exhausted, the four famished hunters sought haven in a restaurant in the village. We ordered hot clam chowder. No one ordered duck.

I set out on a second shooting crusade the next winter, temperature about the same, the salt water frozen around the edges of the bay. After a long vigil, we spotted a gray goose descending. Two of us fired before the bird landed and he soared off contemptuously. And this was called goose hunting! Our leader was an ardent member of Ducks Unlimited, a conservation effort to build up the supply of wild fowl. I wonder how he would have responded if he could have gone hunting with one of the Pilgrims and looked out at those marshes and ponds swarming with birds and no limit on the daily bag. I can just hear him murmuring ecstatically, "paradise."

Shopping with Mother Nature

for September

beach plum

There is no question about it. Homemade jelly and store bought jelly just cannot be compared. The children are gone and we do not need the sweets but we find the excuses just the same to make our favorite wild blackberry jelly. Maybe it is because the berries are hard to find, that we take pride in our achievement or that we enjoy the excursions into nature's solitude. Moreover, we do like to give something to our friends and neighbors at Christmas that they cannot pick up at the supermarket.

One August morning we climbed into our dory anchored in the brook and started paddling upstream, wearing swim suits under our clothes. The blackberries should be ripe. Our two red plastic pails hung at the prow of our small craft. We immediately felt far away from houses, roadways and civilization as we made our way up the meandering stream. It was wilderness quiet, providing a feeling of detachment and exhilaration. The narrow stream drains the ponds and cranberry bogs, carrying their ever-flowing input down to the pond and through its outlet into the Atlantic.

I kept an eye open for brook trout, stocked every spring. The eager fishermen usually hook most of them within a week after the

96

opening day. Trees, brush and weeds crowded the banks, blocking the waterway so that only a canoe or dingy could navigate.

A northern-style jungle flourished along the shores, offering a barrier to landings. Intertwining wild roses, sumac, alders, willows, elderberries and blackberries formed impenetrable thickets. We pulled in close to the overhanging berries, bending with their ripe fruit. They were sweet and juicy and we soon picked enough for jelly making. Almost nobody ventures up the brook anymore since it is nearly impassable to navigation, which keeps our treasure undiscovered.

There is something cheering about shopping with Mother Nature. Her produce is fresh, all natural. No artificial coloring is needed and there is no pirating of one's wallet at the cash register. It is a satisfaction to go directly to the original source without entangling oneself in that intricate net of grower, picker, shipper, marketer, advertiser and merchant.

With our pails full, we steered our way down the brook, shadowed like a narrow lane in Cornwall by the wild growth on the shore. We were soon in the pond, splashing our way through the aquatic weeds that have invaded the once open and clear waters. Having come to the outlet into the ocean, we tied up our dory and walked along the beach to Manomet Point. There are countless stones on this rugged shoreline. The Atlantic coast was described by Francis Parkman as "the shaggy continent from Florida to the Pole, outstretched in savage slumber along the sea."

It is a place of constant fluctuation where tides change as the moon waxes and wanes, where the level of land and sea rises and falls. It is "a stern and rock-bound coast." Tides, undertow and winds play an astute game of banditry, robbing the beaches. The rocks that are swept by wind and foam are covered with Irish moss and brown kelp. The sands are not adorned with shells as in the tropics. They lack the color of the southland. They are prosaic mollusks such as razor clams, soft shell clams, sea clams, quahogs and mussels.

The beach is strewn with sea lettuce, dulce and sargassum. There is no dearth of life and activity in the cool Atlantic, with an abundance of living organisms from barnacles to seals, from horseshoe crabs to whales. Along the high water line we walked among clumps of beachgrass that had rooted in the bleak habitat. Behind them I noted clusters of poverty grass, blue-flowered chicory and yellow dusty miller. The next line of defense included sprawling beach plums that offer blue-purple fruit to jelly makers in September.

We slipped off our slacks and shirts and enjoyed a leisurely swim, the sea gulls dipping above and cheering us on, the salty ozone refreshing us. We dried off and lay for awhile in the warm sunshine, watching the fishing boats. Charlie Snow's dory beached near us. He was coming in from pulling his lobster pots. He lifted up his outboard motor and gave his boat a shove onto the sand. We walked over and poked into a bushel basket full of cherished crustaceans and bought a handsome, wriggling, four-pounder and paddled home with our morning harvest from brook and sea.

On our way Sue outlined our evening meal: boiled lobster, our new potatoes (the first digging), our Kentucky wonder beans (right off their poles), our beefsteak tomatoes (just coming in), blueberry pie (our own berries and Sue's crust made from scratch) and iced tea with our own strawberry mint.

Reaching home, we put the lobster in the refrigerator and changed our beach clothes. Sue started the pie, and I journeyed down the hill to dig potatoes and pick the vegetables. The corn was filling out. Next to the butter and sugar roasting ears was a spread of cucumbers, butternut squash and melons, and then rows of potatoes. I explored a vigorous hill, probing with my hoe to see how much they had grown. It was gratifying to uncover six the size of a silver dollar. I took on another hill and dropped a dozen of the reddish tubers into my woven basket and passed on to the beans.

The Kentucky wonders were hanging in tender green pods from the alder poles I had cut in the spring, set in the ground and surrounded with eight to ten seeds. After a bout with beetles, which I won by patient hand picking, the vines shot up like magic to bear a bounty of our favorites. They outstrip their dwarf cousins in flavor and rank at the top of beandom in my opinion.

Some people like their beans combined with pearl onions, sliced almonds, mushrooms, herbs or even creamed. We prefer them with melted butter, pepper and a pinch of salt. The same with potatoes fresh out of the ground. When one cannot have that

mouth-watering, elemental flavor and must resort to vegetables from the stores, harvested heaven knows when, then one is justified in bolstering them with herbs and sauces.

Just beyond, moving seaward, were cabbages, eggplant and beets. The area devoted to lettuce, peas and other early birds that had played their role, was the bare spot in the garden. I moved on to the tomatoes, tied to their high stakes and mulched with hay and straw. Picking a well-formed "love apple" is almost as exciting as harvesting a peach or an apple. My home nurtured tomatoes shame the pallid specimens from Florida. I have seen them being picked in Collier County, acres and acres of them, to be packed in those tricky pink-colored cellophane wrappers to make them more acceptable to the buyer. Those hard and tasteless billiard balls are not tomatoes, they are phonies.

With my basket full, I headed for the kitchen to share in

preparing a dinner that an Epicurean, who boasts a Croesus bank roll and chefs trained in Paris and Rome, cannot surpass.

Last winter, in Florida, we were invited to an elite dining place in our area. The surroundings were attractive, with palms, flowers, fountains and sunny terraces. The tables were spread with pink linen cloths, set with good china and an ample display of silverware. Male waiters, in natty attire, were eagerly solicitous.

The menu was in French and quite elaborate. I needed my glasses and time to think. There were tempting choices in each category. An appetizer like shrimp crêpe or lobster quiche was $6.95, a cucumber and artichoke soup (four ounces) in a pretty cup was $3.95, a salad of papaya and star fruit was $4.50. An entrée of rack of lamb was $18.95, which the waiter brought in on a large silver tray and deposited on a side table. Then, with great flourish, he cut two very thin ribs and placed them on my plate with three marble-sized potatoes and a tablespoon of stuffed eggplant and quickly whisked the tray elsewhere.

For deserts, the young man recited from memory an overwhelming portfolio of tempting tortes, mousses, bombes, parfaits, pastries, ices and a long list of pies, such as key lime and grasshopper, from $3.50 to $4.50. (For this histrionic performance, his tip should be increased). In final accounting, the bill averaged around $50.00 each.

I am talking about a restaurant in a small town. In New York or other large cities the price would be much higher, depending on the names of the celebrities who patronize the establishment. For those who have money to burn or whose insecurity requires that they be seen in such *haute cuisine* atmosphere, maybe there is some justification. But my conscience will not allow me to pay $50.00 for one dinner when hunger stalks the world. My taste buds dry up at the thought.

By ten o'clock that night I was hungry and Sue caught me in the kitchen slicing a piece of her homemade bread, which I spread with butter and our own blackberry jelly that we brought with us from New England. It was the best item on the day's menu.

An Apple a Day

To bite into a crisp, juicy apple is a gastronomical delight any day of the year. Just think of the comfort and cheer Johnnie Appleseed brought to the homesteaders in the Middle West when he scattered his seed, carried in gunny sacks from New England, around their lonely farm houses.

When we plant a leafless, dry-rooted sapling and nurture it, we are participating in the miraculous creation process that is ongoing and unending. We are replenishing what we have taken from the earth for our sustenance and pleasure, a rewarding endeavor.

All the trees we planted in the late 1930's took hold and flourished. The company included a sweet red cherry, a Queen Ann cherry, a Bartlett pear, two Elberta peaches, a crab apple (for jelly), a Northern Spy, a red Astrachan (for early apple sauce), three Macintosh, three Red Delicious, three Golden Delicious and a Baldwin.

We fertilized, poking holes with an iron bar in a circle under their outermost branches and poured in our orchard mixture. They began bearing the third year. We picked the cherries as fast as they ripened, feasting on them in advance of our avain friends. The peaches were a bon vivant's delight, large, luscious and richly flavored. We indulged ourselves in this rare home grown treat. We ate them fresh off the tree; we had peaches and cream, shortcake and jam. The peach trees lasted, alas, only about twelve years since they are short-lived trees.

Year after year our barn was filled with baskets and boxes of the apple harvest. Our friends picked and carried away a good share of the bounty. The aroma of the pippins brought new life to the old barn, to the beams and rafters that were scarred by wood beetles and worms. In the corner there was usually a mound of bluish grey Hubbard squash, a pile of butternut squash and a circle of golden pumpkins.

The red Astrachan apple was the first to ripen in late summer. It made a delicious red sauce. The famous names came in later. Those who have never reached up to an October sky from a ladder, with their faces touching a red Macintosh and apple fragrance filling the frosty air, have missed a happy adventure. From the crotch of a tree, one holds each globe of beauty in a firm hand, gently twisting to break that tiny stem which has held the fruit since Maytime blossoms faded. Then into a basket it goes.

We carried them to the barn, where we sorted them, picking out the big Macintosh, Golden Delicious and Northern Spies, wrapping them in paper and placing them in layers in boxes. These we moved to the stone cellar of our house where they kept well until past midwinter.

We usually did our main and final picking after two good frosts, which gave added flavor to the fruit. The Macs came in fairly early. They are an all-round apple, possibly the most popular choice for eating as well as for pies and sauce, our favorite. The Golden Delicious is exclusively an eating apple and true to its name. The Northern Spy ranks high for eating, for pies and for long keeping. There is no more satisfying snack any time of the day than apple slices accompanied by crisp crackers and a wedge of cheese.

I love to embark on a pruning expedition. I gather my tools from the barn and tool shed: a strong hand pruner to cut the suckers and a hand saw to slice off the intruding uprights. Everything that grows straight up must go. The tree should be shaped umbrella style. Where branches interlock or rub, one must be cut out. I use my long wooden pruner to reach the high places, pull the wire handle that works the cutter and down comes the excesss growth which consumes the vitality of the tree.

Apples hold their legendary popularity as symbols of the Tree of Life, luring the human hand to reach out and touch their perfection, causing the eyes to contemplate their beauty, the nostrils to breathe the haunting aroma and the tongue to taste the delectable fruit. No wonder Eve was tempted. Apples do not dominate the scene like the oak or the maple. They are satisfied with the outskirts, forming a protective company to cheer and serve. In the spring they offer bending boughs to the bluebirds, song sparrows, wrens and orioles. They provide bowers of pink and white bloom. Then we can watch the evolving nubbins grow into green bulbs and finally into ripening fruit. The red and gold bounty helped carry us through the winter, furnishing us with pies, puddings and sauces.

When the crop has been harvested and the fallen leaves moved to the compost pile, we can look out through frosty windows on the gray bark of twisted and contorting limbs which no other tree can emulate. They ornament our pasture and are a gathering place for winter birds. In our early days with apples, we reaped bumper crops without a spraying program. The new era of insects, worms and fungus diseases dealt us a blow. It became imperative to spray six or eight times a season. We were forced to surrender. Like the trees, we were growing older and we couldn't cope with the complications in our orchard.

The trees revealed considerable spunk in the face of their adversaries, blooming with zest, trying to keep up their former record. The birds did their best to combat moths, caterpillars and beetles which may have heartened the trees a little. Perhaps they were hoping, as we were, that the problems of our habitat would be rectified. We surrendered as gracefully as possible to the inevitable. However, we have not deserted our aging friends. We praise them for their spring performance in which they still play a stellar role, for their gift of shade and their hospitality to the birds that revel in their sweet blossoms.

The orchard company has weathered forty winters. Their fruitful years have come to an end but they carry on as graceful senior citizens in our meadow. They form hardy sentinels during the short days of winter. Sometimes they are shrouded in sparkling snowflakes or bowing low before a sweeping wind. We still groom them, cutting off the gypsy moth eggs and keeping them in shape by pruning so they may grow old gracefully with the feeling of being loved.

Bays, Coves
and Harbors

Tranquility

Plymouth is full of streams and ponds for fishing enthusiasts to enjoy. The brook just below my house is stocked with trout every spring by the Massachusetts Department of Fisheries. On Patriots Day I slipped down to see if I could hook a few of those delectable beauties. It was a tranquil spot. No cars passed on the narrow country road to mar this haven set apart from the busy world and there was no sound except for the sweet voice of a song sparrow in the alder bushes further upstream.

As I stood on the bank under the budding swamp maples and willows, casting onto the surface of the sparkling water, I thought of the patron saint of fishermen, Izaak Walton, and the idyllic accounts he wrote on the romance of fresh water fishing.

He had a glorious time investigating the rivers and lakes of Great Britian. I cannot duplicate his skill as a fly fisherman but I admire his composure. His motto, "Study to be quiet," guided him to many peaceful byways and set him on a ninety year adventure with nature. He kept a firm hold on happiness and a proper perspective upon the vicissitudes of human fortune. When he was seventy, he signed a forty year lease on a house in London and negotiated a loan to repair a property where the dwelling had just burned. Apparently he was not oppressed by the anxieties of old age or the possibility of Father Time's summons to eternity. He was ninety when he drew up his last will and testament.

The *Compleat Angler*, published in 1653, was a popular work. Readers responded to the philosopher fisherman who found peace with his rod, exploring the trout streams, enjoying comradship with nature.

> *Oh the gallant Fisher's life,*
> *It is the best of any,*
> *'Tis full of pleasure, void of strife,*
> *And 'tis belov'd of many:*
> *Other joyes,*
> *Are but toyes,*
> *Only this*
> *Lawful is,*
> *For our skill breeds no ill,*
> *But content and pleasure.*

He wrote of his favorite haunts, the fresh water brooks, rivers, ponds and lakes "whose sweet calm course I contemplate." The English people admired his cheerful philosophy and life style. He shared the company of cultured friends and was close to the Bishop of Winchester Cathedral, where he served as a steward. A memorial was erected in this burial place of the ancient kings after his death in 1683. The poet of the out-of-doors was granted an honored place amoung the princes and knights.

I have visited the area that Izaak Walton loved—the charming pastoral world of South England. All of us who have fished for perch with earthworms on our hooks, all who have flecked a brook with a trout fly, all who have cast a lure far out over a gurgling stream, all who have baited with minnows and sought to outwit a black bass, or trolled for pike or pickerel, or struck a mackerel run, outboard motor foaming the salt water with a silvered spinner trailing, or baited with sea worms and dropped a hand line from a Boston Whaler to the bottom, where the flounders live and feed, form a chorus of admirers, the piscators of generations, who pay tribute to the *Compleat Angler*, our predecessor of the seventeenth century.

I was talking recently with a nurse who has built a cottage in the woods where she can get away from the tenseness of the hospital and be alone with the pines and the birds while fishing in her little pond. She said she had become a better nurse because this refuge had relieved her tensions.

We human beings need the countryside, the mountains, forests, lakes and seashores where we can be quiet, dream dreams and commune with nature.

Chief Seattle, about a hundred years ago, spoke this timely admonition to contemporary man:

> There is no quiet place in the white man's city. No place to hear the unfurling of leaves in spring or the rustle of insects' wings. The clatter only seems to insult the ears. And what is there to life if man cannot hear the lonely cry of the whippoor-will or the argument of the frogs around a pond at night? The Indian prefers the soft sound of the wind darting over the face of a pond, and the smell of the wind itself, cleansed by midday rain or scented with the piñon pine.

Ready About

Holding the tiller while his boat is under full sail is a recreational thrill second to none, our son, Bob, declares. He is a natural seaman. His wife, Virginia, is also an able sailor, and their teenagers, Sandy and Rob, form an expert crew.

The thirty-three foot Pearson Vanguard fiberglass sloop goes by the name of *Camelot III*. She boasts classic lines with a full keel and a nine foot three inch beam which gives her the salty, seaworthy look of the wooden boats. She is equipped with a motor to supplement the sails, if needed, with radio and ship-to-shore telephone and sleeping quarters for six.

She winters in Duxbury and Bob sails her to Cataumet on Cape Cod as early in the season as possible and moors her in Parker's Boatyard. I like to go along on that initial trip. We sail out of Duxbury by Clark's Island, glimpsing the steeples of Plymouth and the harbor that is coming to life with all types of craft tied up between the breakwater and Plymouth Beach.

We head south on Cape Cod Bay, passing Manomet Point and Ellisville off our starboard side, usually encountering brisk winds. It is relaxing to enter the calmer water of Cape Cod Canal and if we have planned wisely in accord with the tide, we will have the current with us from the Sagamore Bridge to the Bourne Bridge. Once in Buzzards Bay, we begin to observe the familiar landmarks that have made the area a favorite haunt of yachtsmen.

Parker's Boatyard is in a protected cove in the northeastern corner of Red Brook Harbor, part of the village of Cataumet. There is no safer place to be during a northeaster or hurricane. Raz Parker operates a hundred or more moorings in the basin, hosting only boats with sails. Raz is a Cape Codder, full of sea talk and knowledge of sailing. He tells motor boats to "get the hell out" of his domain.

Sue and I go down to Cataumet several times during the summer for a sail on *Camelot III*. One day, as we set out on a four-day cruise, the winding outbound channel took us past Bassett's Island where we anchored and swam to the sandy shore to sun bathe and enjoy the warm water.

Back on the boat we had lunch and set sail for Hadley's Harbor, a secluded romantic spot tucked in the northern corner of Naushon island. It is considered by skippers to be one of the loveliest and most secure anchorages on the New England coast.

Buzzards Bay was a world of water, with inlets, coves and harbors shimmering in the sun. Pennants were flying from high masts, horns tooting salutations, sails full of music of the wind, salt spray spilling over the bows and gulls dipping and rejoicing.

There was camaraderie in the air, passing cargoes of waving families in nautical garb, children and dogs, all caught up in a holiday mood, carefree sailors enjoying their home on the water. Their happiness was contagious. It was a pleasure to be alive on such a prime summer day.

Captain Bob operates a tight ship. Sandy and Rob leap about the boat like a couple of young gazelles at his commands, running up the sails, tugging on the lines. Whether they are sunning on the fore deck, grabbing a snack in the galley or dozing in the cockpit, they swing into action like seasoned sailors when Bob shouts at them to pull in the mainsail or check the jib. And when he calls, "Ready about and hard a lee," they duck the swinging boom and make the sheets fast. I watched them with nostalgia as I relaxed in my sheltered corner, remembering that I was once as nimble and carefree. It was a delightful two hour sail.

Hadley's Harbor is not a village. It is an undeveloped natural haven. We entered through a long, winding course. Two sailboats had anchored before us. It was an ideal spot to spend the night. We slipped into our bathing suits, dropped a ladder over the side and eased into the bouyant water. Bob tossed over a couple of brushes and the crew did a clean up job on *Camelot III*. The chore done, we swam ashore and rested on the beach. Gulls, terns and sandpipers were in charge. Returning to the boat, Virginia called excitedly for us to note the whimsical, whiskered face of a harbor seal swimming along beside her.

We dined that evening on lobster salad, rolls and Sue's pound cake. Bunks were made up early. Somnus, god of sleep, was working his magic. Darkness crept around the little harbor. There was no sound from our neighboring sailors. We heard only the soft lapping of the tide against the hull and were soon aleep on Neptune's bosom.

The next morning we sailed out through the channel into the bay and over to Quissett Habor near Woods Hole, about an hour away. The mood of the sea was changing. We were booming along on a close reach, spray flying and sails taut. The breeze was a typical Buzzards Bay sou'wester, known to natives as a Buzzards Bay sleigh ride. The term goes back to whaling days when a harpooned whale sped away with a dory full of sailors.

This area is rich in Indian lore and history of English exploration. Fishing villages grew up along its shores, bearing colorful names like Padanarum, Mattapoisett, Sippiwissett, Angel's Point and Cuttyhunk. Clipper ships and whalers were once familiar sights in these waters.

Quissett is a gem. In our dingy, we took a look at the dock and the shore, rowing among the craft that were tied up at their moorings or anchored for a visit. These post card villages are crowded all summer with boaters who never tire of revisiting them.

Heading south the following day about eleven, we skirted the Elizabeth Islands on our port side before sailing southeasterly through Quick's Hole into Vineyard Sound on our way to Menemsha. There are sixteen of these islands extending like a protecting arm around the southern portion of Buzzards Bay. Most are miniscule. The larger ones are Naushon, Pasque, Nashawena and

Cuttyhunk. Bartholomew Gosnold named this group when he discovered Buzzard Bay in 1602. He recorded in his journal his visit "among these many fair islands."

Impressed by the blossoming grape vines, he gave Martha's Vineyard its name. We were out of sight of land, speeding along. The fretting and stewing that propel me in my work-a-day world are lifted like a weight from my back as I watch the sea around me, the dependability of the tides and the team work of wind and sails. On land I am always striving to alter circumstances. On the ocean I accept the system and follow its rules. I can think without distraction and contemplate the vastness of the waters and the wonders of the universe.

Favorable winds brought us into Menemsha Harbor, an historic fishing hamlet, around two in the afternoon. Tying up was a problem since there were only three moorings, all occupied. A cordial seaman invited us to rack up with him. Enamored with this peaceful spot, we declared a free afternoon. Some roamed about the village and the moors.

Rob and I paid a visit to Captain Rasmus Klimm's Boathouse to buy sea worms so we could fish for flounder from the boat. We came out with our bait and a supply of potato chips and cokes and took our seats on an upturned dory like old sea dogs and contemplated the harbor and the sights and smells around us. The gray shingled boathouse sat on a wind-worn dock and barnacled posts, piled about with mossy lobster traps, bright painted bobber floats and nets draped from walls and dories. Clusters of small sailing craft were gently riding their moorings in Menemsha Pond.

"Neat place," Rob said.

"These are days to remember," I answered.

"Yeah," he added, with a blissful sigh. We watched an old fishing boat chug its way into the harbor. She slowly swung alongside the dock and tied up. The herring gulls that had been dozing on the rooftops were alerted by the arrival of cod and haddock. They started fluttering and squawking as the men unloaded their catch. I followed Rob to the boat to examine the haul.

We set out early the following day for Edgartown on the southeast corner of the Vineyard. The famous whaling harbor was once alive with tall ships and lionhearted crews who sailed the far seas in search of whale oil. Today only the memories of those heroic days remain in the popular summer capital of the island that now bulges with affluent residents and visitors.

In the Dukes County Historical Society we viewed one hundred daguerreotypes of local sea captains who commanded many of the ships that set forth from Edgartown, Nantucket and New Bedford. I can picture the excitement as they sailed out of the harbor on a voyage around the Horn, bound for the Orient or a trip to the South Seas or the Arctic. And I think of the tumultuous welcome when a whaler put into the harbor after months at sea, the hold filled with sperm oil to light the lamps of New England.

Sue could never pass an antiques shop without "just a peek." She came back happy with a tin hogscraper candlestick, "just right for the fireplace mantel," she said.

We broiled swordfish that evening on the charcoal grille off the stern. A hungry gull circled the boat, swooping down to seize a slice and take off with its catch. I grabbed a long fork and stood guard to ward off other pirates. It was an unforgettable feast enjoyed in the rosy light of the sunset with French bread, Vineyard tomatoes and cool Chablis.

Tommorrow we would return to Parker's Boatyard and start dreaming about the next cruise in the waters around my corner of New England with their endless attractions.

Ballet Dancers of the Sea

Whale watching has become popular the past few seasons along our shores. I took a short cruise in Massachusetts Bay on Captain John's sturdy deep sea fishing boat last week. The sun and the cottony clouds in an azure sky were staging the setting for an ideal summer day. The second hour, when we were well out, we spotted humpback whales surfacing about a quarter of a mile away. I felt a shiver of fear as I watched the monarchs of the deep, thinking of Captain Ahab and Moby Dick and the age-old feud between man and whale, the gory encounters, the butchery and barbarism recorded in the annals of whaling.

In those days of man, the marauder, we would have climbed into a dory, harpoon in hand, and pursued the ancient and honorable masters of the sea, bent on destruction. It appears to me that we may be emerging into a new era as far as whale rights are concerned. Maybe we are beginning to honor their claim to a peaceful existence in the kingdom where they have ruled for centuries.

On our return, a little closer to shore, we saw dolphins sporting their skill in the blue-green waters. These jovial cousins of the whale family are my favorites. It thrills me to see them roll, plunge and soar. As the marine jet set, they are always ready to stage a happy hour. These playboys and playgirls revel in their fun-loving life style.

I have watched them from shipboard on the Pacific, Atlantic and Mediterranean, where they never failed to attract fascinated spectators. They are like gamboling lambs, blithe and carefree, stirring envy among the munching cows and lethargic humans. Their exuberance is spectacular, their *joie de vivre* a rebuke to the cynical, as they play together and race sailboats and motorboats. They leap in the sea, splashing silvery spray, plunging below the surface to rise again in their cavorting.

These performers steal the show in every zoo and marine-land. They quite overwhelm us with their open-hearted trustfulness and sociability. They forget that we are their historic enemies. They chirp cheerfully as they eat from our hands, stand on their tails and leap skyward with that built-in smile on their beak-like snouts.

The bottlenosed dolphins have returned for centuries to home bases like Penngu, Taiwan to feed on squid and octopus. They travel at a speed of thirty-seven miles an hour and devour twenty percent of their body weight each day in fish in order to maintain their intense schedule. When they stage their annual homecoming to Taiwan, the local fishermen carry out their hunt and restock their supply of meat and oil.

A Taiwanese, Steven Shieh, was touched by the hardship of the dolphins at the hands of the fisherfolk. He enlisted financial aid and bought captured victims, saved them from execution, placed them in sea pens, trained them in new skills and sold them to scientific institutions and marinelands. He demonstrated the capabilities of his pupils and succeeded in breeding them in captivity.

Graduates of his dolphin academy were soon performing in the Hong Kong Marine Park. Shieh recently shipped twenty-one of his protégés on a charter flight of a German cargo plane to Frankfort, Marseilles and Switzerland. They are now engaged in sonar research under the direction of Professor G. Busnel of the *Laboratorie d'Acoustie Animale* of France. Before departing, the dolphins were given a beauty treatment, their bodies rubbed with oil to keep their skin from drying. They were then placed in suspended cradles on the plane and sprayed with salt water all the way of their thirty hour journey to Frankfort.

The sonar system of the dolphins is being studied by scientists who try to adapt it for use in nuclear submarines. The U.S. Navy in Hawaii is researching their capacity to swim and dive. One achieved a dive of 1,700 feet.Experiments indicate they can serve as search instruments to locate lost objects, wrecked ships and retrieve valuable items from the sea. Their brains can solve problems and sustain interest in projects for an extended period of time. They have been used as life guards, employing their sonar to rush to the aid of a swimmer in need, offering their dorsal fin to a human and towing him ashore.

The word porpoise is used broadly to include dolphins, although they are chubbier and smaller than their cousins. Some porpoises swim with ships, but they are more snub-nosed and do not have the mouth construction that creates the built-in smile. One dolphin named Pelorous Jack acted as a pilot for the New Zealand ships at Pelorous Sound for twenty-five years. He would appear when the ship's whisle sounded, assume his post and guide the vessel through the shoals on her daily trip.

In 1909 Jack did not show up and the *Pegasus* was wrecked with all seventy-five passengers lost. He had been injured by the ship's propeller and swam off to recuperate. He returned after the calamity and piloted other ships until he disappeared in 1912.

To look into the pensive eyes of these marine stars is to reflect on how they have already probed sonar mysteries and the unexplored depths of the sea. I can understand why the Greek legend affirmed the dolphins had once been part of the human race. One million years ago they left the land for the ocean. Some believe that they return to the land when they feel the premonition of death, going back to the area where they were born and where their ancestors lived.

Clamming

When I tug on my rubber boots, pick up my rake and bucket, I move to the low tide beach and find myself in a new marine world. Only a few hours before I had been floating here in Duxbury Bay in the warm summer waters, on my back, looking blissfully at the cloudless sky, swimming out to a Boston Whaler at its moorings. Now, later in the day, the tides have performed a change, offering another beach setting.

How could all that water move so quietly out to sea, revealing a wide expanse of stony, black soil well pebbled with small rocks, with bits of eel grass and kelp on top? I saw two confused horseshoe crabs that were caught in the transformation and little sand crabs scurrying about among the rocks, which must look like mountains to their tiny eyes.

When I swim there I often wear light rubber shoes to protect my feet. I learn to chip away with my rake, snatching up the gray shells from their humble estate. They are covered with clinging black mud. This obstacle tends only to increase their sweetness and can be washed safely away by a little dipping in the bay and a final rinsing in the kitchen sink.

The soft shells have staked out their homesteads on the flats of marshes, inlets and bays along the shoreline where the tides come and go. They are stationary dwellers who live and feed in the sand and mud, opening their shells and sticking out their rubbery necks, gleaning the nourishment they need from their unromantic environment. Yet here in the muck are generated one of the delicacies of seafood.

These denizens of the darkness live under the beach where human feet tramp and gulls and terns forage, below the water and sand. They have developed the habits of hermits. "Tight as a clam," we say. Their shell is their only protection. They don't gypsy around like some creatures, evict tenants from their property or move into abandoned houses.

The soft shells are the most sought after by clam diggers. After rinsing, we place them in a large pot with a cup of water and steam until they open their shells, just a few minutes. They are seldom used commercially for chowder due to the high price they bring. The restaurants use the big sea clams.

Further out on the sea bottom are the hard shell clams, the chaps that refuse to open up for you without a tussle with a sharp knife. They can be picked up by rake or by ducking down and grabbing one. They are eaten raw on the shell or gound up, mixed with eggs, cracker crumbs, butter and pepper and baked in their shells. We like Cape Cod delight—a baked quahog casserole. Still further out in the bay are the deep sea clams. These big fellows can be gathered only at extra-low tide. Three or four of them, ground up, will make a tasty chowder or a delicious dish baked in the shells.

I am impressed as I poke around the clam world with the order that prevails. It is a remarkable sea empire that gives one a sense of the evolutionary process developed by countless forms of aquatic life. Clams are only one item in the marine inventory. Many land creatures have made the ocean their birthplace, slowly evolving into amphibians or land animals.

I think of the tides that set the rhythm for diversity of habits and movements of every inhabitant from protozoa to whale. Ocean life is complex, like earth life. The system has worked for aeons of time. And this guides me back to that orderly change ever in process, organisms evolving from pre-existing forms. Naturalists call it evolution. So do philosophers and historians. So do many theologians. Evolution is the process of orderly change.

I share with Harlow Shapley, the Harvard astronomer, the wonder that stirred his mind as he studied the natural order:

> The new discoveries and developments contribute to the unfolding of a magnificent universe; to be a part thereof and participant therein is also maginificent. With our confreres on distant planets; with our fellow plants and animals of land, sea and air on this planet; with the rocks and waters of all planetary crusts; and the atoms and protons that make up the stars — with all these we are associated in an existence and an evolution that inspires respect and deep reverence. We cannot escape humility. And as groping philosophers and scientists we are grateful for the mysteries that still lie beyond our present grasp.

I have dug clams at Corn Hill on the narrow spit of earth called Truro, down on Cape Cod. The soil there was as black and mucky as in Duxbury, but there were no stones to contend with. I could see the pin holes in the sand, which indicated that a clam was down below. I tapped with the handle of my rake. If there was a tenant, it sent up a squirt of water, and down I went after it. The clams were ideal, sizable, plump and lively.

The Pilgrims didn't realize what choice food was waiting here for them. They were hungry for beef, lamb and good bread and unfamiliar with what the shell fish had to offer. They did find some Indian corn in this area which gave the place its name, Corn Hill.

What a restful spot on an autumn day, when the tourists had departed and Indian summer held the precious bit of earth in its embrace. And what an evening followed, with genuine New England chowder made of clams, fresh from Cape Cod Bay.

This is how we make clam chowder:

1. Slice and chop very fine about a 2-inch square piece of salt pork and try it out slowly in a frying pan until brown and crispy. Drain and set aside.

2. Peel 6 or 7 potatoes and cut in small cubes. Place in a 3 quart pan with a minimum of water (about 2½ cups). Add one large finely shredded onion to the potatoes and ¾ teaspoon

of salt. *Cover* and simmer until potatoes are barely done. They must not be too soft. Never pour off water. (This is the reason for using as little water as possible.)

3. Squash out the black residue from the stomachs of one quart of clams. Do this with your two thumbs and your two forefingers. (This is quick and easy and less wasteful of the clams than trying to cut them out.) Chop off about ½ of the clam necks. Now chop the clams slightly. Save all the clam liquor. Place clams and liquor in pan with ¼ cup of water and simmer 3 minutes. Don't boil!

4. Add ¾ quart whole milk and one pint of cream to the cooked potatoes and onions. Next add clams, 2 to 3 tablespoons of the pork crispies and 2 tablespoons of butter. Stir gently until mixed. Bring to simmer and remove at once from fire. Add black pepper and serve with pilot crackers and pickles. Use chef's judgment on adding a little more or less milk or potatoes. Whatever is left over will taste even better the next day. Evaporated milk, diluted to taste, may be substituted for fresh milk and cream.

Island of Refuge

Clark's Island, roughly eighty acres in size, lies in Duxbury Bay about three miles from the shore. It is covered with scrub oak, pine, cedar and dense shrubbery entangled with wild blackberries. It was a dark and desolated spot on December 20, 1620 when sixteen men from the *Mayflower* shallop were blown off course in a raging storm and landed on her shore. Their mast was broken, sails torn and rudder damaged. They were soggy wet with sleet, snow and salt spray, hungry and exhausted. A short distance inland they found the Great Rock and in its shelter built a fire to dry their clothes and warm themselves. They passed a miserable night, huddled together, not knowing where they were.

They had left the *Mayflower* in Provincetown and were searching for a suitable place to locate. The next day was Sunday. The sun broke through and they decided to keep the Sabbath. Govenor Carver probably led them in this simple act of worship, assisted by Bradford and Winslow. This was the first recorded Christian service in New England.

If the shallop had gone down with these sixteen leaders, the *Mayflower* passengers and crew might have perished on the tip of

Cape Cod. Their names will be remembered as long as there is an America. They are: Govenor John Carver and his servant, John Howland, Myles Standish, William Bradford, Edward Winslow, John and Edward Tilley, Richard Warren, Stephen Hopkins and his servant, Edward Doty, the pilot, John Clark, Robert Coppin, the master gunner and three sailors whose names are not listed.

On Monday, having repaired their boat, they sailed to Plymouth where they found fresh water and cultivatable land and decided to settle there. They returned to Provincetown and brought the *Mayflower* over. On Christmas Day they went ashore, "some to fell timber, some to saw, some to rive and some to carry, so no man rested all day."

William Bradford recorded in his journal:

> That which was most sad and lementable was that in two or three months time half of their company died, especially in January and February being the depth of winter and wanting houses and other comforts; being infected with scurvy and other diseases which this long voyage and their inaccommodate conditions had brought upon them. So there died two or three a day in the aforesaid time, that of 100 odd persons, scarce fifty remained.

He challenged those who would come after:

> May not and ought not the children of these fathers rightly say 'our fathers were Englishmen who came over this great ocean and were about to perish in this wilderness but they cried unto the Lord and He heard their voice and looked on their adversity.'

The island has continued to be a haven of refuge. The herring gulls and black back gulls discovered its peaceful seclusion and made it their major nesting place. They took over the northern part years ago. The herons followed them and established one of their chief North American breeding centers. Nature has provided isolation from the rest of the world by a nine foot tide, shallows and sandbars. There is no harbor inlet, so that it is possible to land only for a two or three hour period at high tide.

In 1971, the snowy egrets moved in to set up their colony. Song birds also abound and feast on the wild berries. The sky has been alive with birds every time I have visited the island. I have circled their habitat in a launch as they swam and flew about me. They have created a successful refuge in the spot that gave shelter to the sixteen shipwrecked men in their distress. The presence of these seabirds helps keep the island a place of natural beauty. What more fitting monument to the Pilgrims!

There are no obelisks or statues, no signs, caretakers or guides to interpret the story. But each summer the Duxbury people remember and come to the island of refuge with their friends and children in a little regatta of Boston Whalers, open launches, power boats and sailing vessels. They spread their picnic lunches on the grass and later assemble at the Great Rock to retell the Clark's Island epic.

When the Fog Comes In

Fog is unpredictable, even for the expert weathermen. It shows up in the spring, summer, fall and winter. Also it can come morning, noon or night. Fog is a torment to fishermen and pleasure sailors but a boon to crops and flowers in the dry season.

Yesterday morning was cloudy and hazy. Around noon, the air grew heavy with moisture and the fog began settling in around the barn. The gold horse weathervane was lost to view. The mist tumbled into the orchard and up the hill to wrap itself protectingly about the house. It was a gentle invasion of vapor condensed from particles of water suspended over the face of the earth. It differs from clouds only in being on the ground.

Balm from the Atlantic refreshed the creatures of field and woods. Flowers bathed their faces in the moist haze and lifted their wilted heads. Frequent fog accounts for the superlative blossoms of the British Isles and the pink-cheeked girls.

I stood for a moment by a front window in my study, peering out on a road shrouded in silence and anonymity. Neighboring houses were swallowed up in the void. I turned to the east window in the keeping room and tried to locate the barn. It was not there.

Even the maple beside the house had been impaled. All landmarks had disappeared. Sue looked in the refrigerator. Provisions were low. Whether one is king in the counting house or the maid in the garden, one is unable to move until the fog, in its own good time, decides to leave.

Later in the day, when the fog had lifted a trifle, I took a walk with Candy through the orchard. The spider webs in the grass were luminous with silver sheen. The silk spinners had been busy all summer casting their lines from limb to limb to provide intercommunication and transfer of their captured insects. Their handiwork formed an impressive display of engineering and artistic creativity.

Candy considered fog another adventure with nature. She liked its cooling touch on her whiskers and nose. Her coat glistened with tiny droplets of moisture. The complexity a sailor faces does not put a golden retriever off course. With her sixth sense she is sure of her directions.

The rhythmic sigh of the foghorn from the Gurnet gives us warning. If I am in bed when I hear this sound, I dream of sea voyages and feel the roll of the ship and the pulse of the engines. Today our system of radar protection brings a degree of security unknown to former sailors. Inventive brains have revolutionized the science of navigation, countering in large measure the danger seamen face.

Winter fog sometimes presages a thaw and is welcomed as a moderator. It sucks up snowdrifts and the dangling icicles like a wet sponge, freeing the soil from the weight it has been patiently bearing. The deep freeze is broken, affording a respite for taking inventory on what the balance of winter may offer. Better a foggy day in winter, I say, than a sleet and ice storm or a northeaster.

We were out last summer in Duxbury Bay in a Boston Whaler linefishing for flounder with sea worms for bait. Looking back at the Bug Light, we could see a fog cloud forming. We were several miles from our moorings. Our skipper wisely pulled anchor and we started bumping the gentle waves, heading for our spot at the Yacht Club. It was a close race with the fog pushing us from behind, every minute piling curtains of impenetrability, reaching forward like an octopus to engulf us. It was a tense encounter between a cockleshell boat and this silent, stealthy force swallowing up everything in its path. We made it that time, but we could have been befogged in the bay for hours. The sailor must keep a sharp eye on nature's changing moods.

On sea and highway this vaporous enemy is a threatening force, admonishing us to be cautious. When at home, and there is no need to venture forth, I find the ozone-laden air soothing and relaxing. I put away my garden tools and shut the shed and garage doors when I see the first wave of fog creeping upstream along the brook and rolling over the meadow. The chores of outside work are laid aside. It is time to call it a day, to slide into one's slippers, head for a comfortable chair and the new flower and vegetable catalog.

Oysterin'

We have a salty friend in Wellfleet on Cape Cod. I remember him as I first met him, in hip boots, oilskin weather gear, yellow rain hat pulled down over a heavy thatch of gray hair, with the strap tight under his firm jaw. He has been oysterin' for fifty years. We take a trip down the Cape every fall after "the people" have departed and the oysters are in.

The early morning ride from the Canal down old Route 6A avoids the Mid-Cape Highway and leads us through those unspoiled seaside villages. We know every house and shop from Sandwich to Provincetown. We still debate as we mosey along about our favorite old inns, antiques dealers, spots for picnicking, fishing, swimming and dune walking. There is the glass museum in Sandwich by the water mill, the tree-shaded center of Yarmouth, the green in Dennis, Pleasant Bay between Orleans and Chatham, the ancient windmill in Eastham, the rugged shore cliffs in Wellfleet, the hill churches of Truro and a sandy point called Provincetown, where the Pilgrims first came ashore.

All along the way are inlets, harbors, sailboats, white cottages, steepled churches, scrub pine, lilacs, climbing roses, lilies and hydrangeas, with gulls shrilling their welcome. Tables, set in front of green-shuttered cottages and sea captains' houses display beach plum jelly for sale. Beach plum jelly and Cape Cod go together like lobsters and Maine. We used to pick them along the edges of the woods, brooks and ponds and counted it a lost fall if we didn't "do up" at least fifty glasses. They have become harder to find like many other of nature's wild friuts.

But this time we must concentrate on the village of Wellfleet. Capt'n Rich greeted us at his gray-shingled oyster shack, perched on an inlet in the harbor, famous for its warm swimming and for its oysters and scallops. Sue and I spent two summer vacations in the village before we acquired our place in Plymouth. I agree with Thoreau that the Cape begins at Orleans and grows more distinctive as one moves toward the tip. My favorite spots are Wellfleet and Truro, where the land narrows to a mile or so in width and is bathed by the swells of the Atlantic on the east and the waves of Cape Cod Bay on the west.

The peaceful harbor of Wellfleet is without equal, offering ideal sailing, with protected waters for swimming that rival any of the south shore towns of the Cape. The village was called Whale Fleet in the days of harpoons and whale hunters. It was not difficult to picture a sailing ship at anchor in this harbor, with a dory bringing crew members ashore to walk the sandy streets among the white houses, lighted by whale oil and bayberry candles.

I fell in love at first sight with the water front and the dwellings that had been built among the gentle hills and valleys. During my happy ramblings I explored the salt water rivers and marshes, the ponds and the rugged back shore with its wild surf, steep cliffs and sand dunes. I noted the wind-swept kettles and kames and their springy checkerberry carpet, amazed at the flora that flourished on this slender finger of earth which had its birth, like Venus, out of the sea.

In the early days the Congregational Church was the religious center of Wellfleet and the spiritual home of the first families. When the Methodists appeared on the Cape, they were called "the Late Comers." The "First Comers" ignored them as a transitory sect and refused to grant them use of the church burying ground. Under pressure, the deacons put up a fence, setting apart the lower, less desirable portion for the final resting places of John Wesley's flock.

This was one of the controversies that troubled the otherwise bucolic Wellfleet during whaling days. But it was a mild disturbance compared with the locust invasion of "the summer people" and the new Cape Highway. Fortunately, the town has preserved much of its original charm in its old houses, its harbor, beaches and its incomparable oysters.

Capt'n Rich's wife and Sue took off on an expedition to gather meadow rue and bittersweet for winter wreaths and bouquets. I climbed aboard with the Captain and the battered boat plowed away from the church spires, the bronzed oaks and brown marshes, rolling slightly in the crisp October air. While nursing the motor and setting his course, he pointed to some wooden stakes a distance from shore, "heading out there to the oyster beds."

After tossing in the anchor, he seized a pair of long-handled nippers with biting teeth at the base and poked them over the gunwales. His rugged hands pressed the pinchers of the giant tongs together. Closing on the shellfish below, he tugged the haul upward, shell, sand and seaweed, dumping his catch on the deck. The tongs continued to heap up the harvest of the sea, scraping the boat side, opening their clamped jaws to drop another hillock of gray shells.

Under the Captain's direction, I picked out kelp, crabs and dry shells. "Dead shells go back for clutch," he said. "We lay them out at breeding time. The water is cloudy with spat when male and female connect. We plant the spat over the shells and hope it will find a home in the beds."

After an hour of pulling anchor and shifting hunting grounds, Capt'n Rich was satisfied with his catch. He had an order for the party that evening at the Yacht Club. How lucky these guests would be! I have tasted oysters in many parts of the world but never any to compare with those from the waters of Wellfleet Harbor.

Chugging back on the *Mary Rich*, he took out his oyster knife. "I'll shuck a few now." He thrust in the blade at the soft spot, liberating the staunchly anchored hermit. I tipped up the shell and the cold, tangy flavor, cherished by gourmets from Canton to Paris, slipped down, tantalizing my taste buds, an ample reward for my adventures in oysterdom. We tied up at the dock in front of the Oyster House with small mountains of shells around it.

We carried in the metal baskets mounded with the briny catch. The Captain whetstoned his knife and started on the first pile of bivalves. He picked up a horny specimen, slit it deftly, sliding the oyster from its fortress into a quart container, tossing the shell into a galvanized can. "Ought to shuck a half dozen for each guest," he estimated. "They expect around sixty at the party tonight. That's 360." Nonchalantly, he proceeded to face the harvest of the day piled about him, each armored mollusk a challenge to his unerring tool.

Corn Roast on the Beach

"Memory is given us that we may gather roses in December," wrote James M. Barrie. One of the happy memories of our early years in Plymouth, when the children were young, is the annual corn roast on the beach. One year we had not only a bumper harvest of corn, but also an abundance of other vegetables, melons and raspberries. Our pantry shelves were filled with rows of canned beans, beets, peas, corn, tomatoes, cucumber pickles and raspberry jam.

I was thinking as I came up from the garden that particular day, toting a burlap bag full of roasting ears, that this was the best crop in a long time. There were no borers, no worms. The grains were full grown, yet oozing milk when pressed. They were our favorite — golden bantam.

We were on our way to a corn roast and since we were the only growers in the gang, we were expected to produce enough luscious maize for fourteen hungry mouths. Pulling the ears was the very last chore. The corn must be fresh. The car was already loaded and in the driveway, packed with thermos jugs of ice tea and lemonade, food hampers containing hamburgers and hot dogs, ketchup, mustard, pickles, Sue's famous potato salad, fresh tomatoes, sliced cucumbers and a twenty-five pound watermelon.

Our cavalcade unpacked at the chosen spot, just before Eel River flows into the ocean. Plymouth Beach is a barrier reef that reaches out three miles into the harbor. It was formed by the tides and storms through the centuries and is shaped like a leg of mutton, widening as it extends toward the end. The blown sands support a few hardy shrubs like beach peas, seaside golden rod, sea rocket and beach roses. The broad terminus has been set aside as a bird preserve.

During the nesting season, a variety of terns take over, hovering in a flutter of white and then plunging into the sea for fish. Snowy egrets, on their long, black legs, feed in the marshes and tidal flats. Thousands of gulls that nest on nearby Clark's Island hunt and relax here. Plovers and sandpipers visit the beach each year on their flights from the arctic to the southern hemisphere.

Following an exploration of the beach, the elders engaged in master planning while the young fry blew off steam and ran wild, getting reacquainted after a time of separation. This was an annual get-together of three families, life-long friends—a doctor, a professor, a minister, their wives and eight offspring.

We caught up on the news, supervised the usual foot races and soft ball, enjoying the sea air and the evening beauty. With cries of "When do we eat?", the fire was laid, the long-handled hamburg cookers made ready and sticks for frankfurts. I kept watching for the coals to accumulate before laying the unshucked ears of corn and covering them with hot ashes. We set up a portable table to keep the edibles from contact with the sand.

We were ravenous. Everything tastes better on the edge of the sea. Round two of hamburgers and hot dogs was underway when the treat of the evening was produced. Tender green ears roast quickly. We had first soaked them in salt water and wiped them with a beach towel before laying them on the coals. We used an old pair of fireplace tongs to lift out samples and test progress, making sure they didn't overcook. We laid the finished product on the table stripping off the husks. The juniors rushed in and grabbed a prize, rolled it in a platter of butter and proceeded to devour it, sliding it back and forth like a harmonica player, from ear to ear, enjoying a treat available only to those who grow their own. I pity the innocent shoppers who pick up a packet of "fresh" corn in the supermarket, shucked and sealed in cellophane.

We watched two large white vessels that were maneuvering in the gathering darkness about a mile off shore. A teenager asked, "Are they warships? Are they German spies?" I ventured to guess that they were menhaden fishing boats that catch small herring-like fish to manufacture oil for use in industry. My surmise was supported by Uncle Gene. The boats, with their lights twinkling like stars, afloat on the dark bosom of the ocean, moved in slow circles as if sweeping the water with their nets. The fanciful spectacle carried our thoughts out to sea. Everyone was guessing how far it was to Provincetown and how far to England and Spain.

The watermelon had been cut. It was a long oval striper from Texas. Sue had picked it out. She knew how to size them up, to smell them and thump them to see if they went "punk." If so, they were ripe. The marshmallows were being roasted on long willow sticks, offering that last sweet tidbit.

Uncle Leighton suggested that we have some stories and there was a call for Sue to tell her folk tale about Mr. Frog. She could slip into the southern dialect in a flash. She told us how the little brown bird was singing in the willow above the pond when Mr. Frog lost his heart to her. He croaked from the muddy bank: "Will you marry me? Will you marry me?" And the little brown bird chirped back: "Yes, I will. Yes, I will."

But Mr. Frog was in no hurry to set the wedding date, and when the little brown bird kept asking when the wedding day would be, Mr. Frog always croaked: "Let's put it off 'til you come from the North."

Finally the pretty little wren got tired of the vascillator and said she would never marry him and she was lucky to lose him and flew to a tree on the other side of the pond.

Mr. Frog was mighty sorry when he knew he had lost the little wren and is sorry till yet. He can still be heard croaking sadly in the pond: "O, I wish I had. I wish I had. I wish I had."

The little brown bird flies a little higher in the tree and chirps: "Well, you could, but you wouldn't. You could, but you wouldn't."

"The moral, children, is when you have a good thing in your

hand, don't let it slip through your fingers." Of course Sue told it with her own dramatic intepretation and the crowd screamed for more.

Someone shouted, "Now let's hear from the children." We had taught ours to memorize poems and short stories and recite them at family gatherings. In our childhood Friday afternoons at school were given over to singing and "speaking pieces" of wide variety from "Captain, my captain" to "the quality of mercy is not strained." The ear and the tongue were trained in classical language. This cultural exposure has been eliminated from the public school system. There is neither interest nor time for such refinements. Elementary school children must discuss ethnic conflicts, minority rights and sex education.

There was the usual holding back and "you go first." After due prodding, the youngsters took their posts, one by one, beside the dying embers of the fire. We heard "I wandered lonely as a cloud," "Little lamb, who made thee?" and "They go down to the sea in ships" and a couple of Ben Franklin's proverbs. Some of the less forensic exhibited their prowess by turning handsprings, doing cartwheels and yodeling.

Five year old Bob, the youngest, finally got up enough courage to "say his piece." He stood stiff as a soldier, arms straight down by his sides, thumb and finger of his right hand twisting the hem of his shorts, and bellowed in rapid fire speed: "If a task is once begun, never leave it 'till it's done. Be a labor great or small, do it well or not at all." He got a big hand.

All in all, the talent would have done credit to a Redpath Chautauqua program. Then Aunt Harriet said: "How about some songs?" She set us off on "My bonnie lies over the ocean" and we swung into "Sailing, sailing over the bounding sea." Our little glee club sang on into the night, harmonizing on old time melodies, drawing on the hymn book and winding up with "Merrily we roll along."

Uncle Gene turned our eyes in a reverent search for the North Star and then together we boxed in the Great Dipper and the Little Dipper. We cast about for Venus and lost ourselves in the glory of the Milky Way. "How close we are to the sky tonight!" a youthful voice whispered.

We followed the usual ritual of saying farewell to the fire, covering the last embers with their blanket of sand. We collected our paraphernalia, slipped on our sneakers and moved quietly across the beach to our waiting cars. Someone was singing softly, "Sweet and low, wind of the western sea."

Broad Margins

A Broad Margin of Leisure

Hosea Prince has been gone for many years, but when we first arrived in the mid-1930s he sold the best clams and lobsters one could buy, as his father had done before him. Hosea lived a few miles south on a dirt road winding off the highway to a salt water inlet. His house was an old salt box. The roof of the long ell sagged. Most of the faded yellow paint had peeled and crumbled to the ground. For three summers ladders had been leaning against the front of the dwelling and neighbors conjectured that Hosea was about to start a paint job. But he just couldn't get around to it.

When I stopped to buy a quart of shucked clams one day, I found Hosea in the back yard, sitting in a slat-back chair, smoking his pipe. Around him was a collection of semi-antiquities, old enough for the town dump, but not good enough to make a second-hand shop. There was a blue painted wagon, minus a wheel, a dilapidated chair swing, the skeleton of a Ford car, a pile of lobster pots and two battered dories, bottom sides up and a barn where he kept his refrigerator and lobster tank.

I never saw Hosea without his white boating cap tipped back on his head of fading red hair. He was usually clad in khaki trousers, a plaid shirt and either rubber boots or sneakers. The ruddy cheeks and lanky figure gave the impression of complete relaxation and freedom from worries about getting ahead in the world that activate and drive most of us. I envied his composure and contentment in the life style he had developed in his spot on the tranquil arm of Cape Cod Bay.

Hosea knew where the clams were to be found when he could summon enough energy to pick up his rake and bucket and get his beat up truck started and rattle off to the diggings. It was never safe to drop in to buy shell fish but he had no telephone and one had to take the chance. Fortunately that day he had some merchandise, already shucked and in his wooden ice box. Summers he clammed and lobstered. Winters he rested. He managed to make a go of it out of his harvest from the sea and produce from his garden.

He was one who shared the outlook of Thoreau:

> My greatest skill is to want but little. I am convinced that to maintain one's self on this earth is not a hardship, but a pastime, if we live simply and wisely. It is not necessary that a man should earn his living by the sweat of his brow, unless he sweats easier than I do.

I drove often to his place for clams and lobsters and to chat with a man who knew what he wanted in life. One day I found him relaxing on a bench in front of his house, facing the salt water inlet, brimming with a full tide, with herring gulls hovering over the browning grass. A patch of goldenrod flamed along the water's edge, just beyond the narrow dirt road that pased in front of the leaning picket fence. It was one of those halcyon September days that steal their way into New England autumn.

A buddy was seated beside him. Two salts had been enjoying sea talk. Hosea invited me to sit down, pointing to a dismantled buggy seat with a frayed horsehair cushion. He was saying that he had been offered a job of painting a big summer place on the Bluffs that belonged to a New York couple. It was mighty good money but he passed it up because he might have to pay income tax, he explained.

I never heard Hosea in such a loquacious mood. Perhaps it was the result of empty beer cans beside him. "I was talking with Bud

Nickerson the other day," he went on. "I asked how he made out this summer at the Blue Whale Inn," Hosea took plenty of time with his words as he whittled on the butt end of a shingle. "Bud said that he ain't never made enough to quit, and he ain't never lost enough to quit, but come next year he hopes to the Lord that he will do one or the other."

I reminded Hosea that Sue was waiting for some two pound lobsters. He said he was all out but had a jumbo in the tank that would weigh about six or seven pounds and I could have it for a couple of bucks.

Hosea wasn't exactly a ne'er-do-well. He just worked when it was necessary. To encounter a person who can make a living without sweating is rare. I don't imagine there have been too many of them since the time of Thoreau. I doubt if Hosea had read the Walden sage but he upheld his statement that "a broad margin of leisure is beautiful in a man's life as it is in a book." I feel constrained to add here that neither Thoreau nor Hosea had a wife or child to support.

Finding the Sunny Spot

On the whole I think I have an optimistic nature, but now and then I fall into the clutches of the Depression Syndrome. I read about Gaddafi and his Libyan hit squad and Castro's liberation corps organizing their revolution in every nook and corner of the globe. My antagonism to dictators turns my thoughts to the Kremlin. When I was first there the images and statues of Stalin were still omnipresent but Khrushchev was beginning to sound off minor blasts against the tyrant. And on my second visit, the posters and statuary had disappeared and so had Khrushchev. This reassured me a bit. The tyrants have their day and cease to be.

I was angry when Mao Zedong teamed up with Stalin and started imprisoning and exiling the freedom seekers of China. Maoism endured for three decades, a long period even for patient China. "The mills of the gods grind slowly but they grind exceeding small."

These reflections, back flashes in time, help me work out of my depression. I begin to measure contemporary bullies against the background of nature, the order that contrasts with disorder. I think of these braggarts in light of the structure that lies back of human behavior, the moral rules that have been established through experience. Despots like Napoleon and Hitler must fail. The primal laws cannot be violated forever.

This philosophical rationalizing may be a slender comfort to some, but it does detour me from the bog of despair to the testimony of history, which drags villain after villain across the stage and dumps them in their graves. The onward march of right may be temporarily halted by oppression, but candles will glow again in the cells of scholars and truth will be proclaimed from pulpits of the prophets. The globe in its orbit moves on. The stars summon men to look up. The streams that foam and flood the land are absorbed in the eternal sea. Nature speaks to distraught humans about hope and renewal.

The Chinese philosophers learned centuries ago that certain established rules exist and the superior man respects them. The earth is under the rule of heaven. The sage keeps in tune with the will of heaven. Confucius taught that there was a cosmic order or course of nature called the *Tao*. Commune with this spirit of heaven, he said. Study the harmony of nature and this will promote harmony in the family and in society.

Lao tzu also spoke of the *Tao*, the eternal way that pervades nature. He thought of the *Tao* as the beginning of heaven and earth, as the first principle. "I am on my knees," he said, "before creative nature." Basic rules have been worked out through thousands of years, forming a dependable structure for the universe.

There is usually a sunny spot to be found in spite of the dark clouds that hover over and around us. Our daughter's dog, Rags, stayed with us while Mary was taking a summer course in Appalachian music at Berea College last summer. Mary paid two dollars for Rags at the pound nineteen years ago when Rags was six months old. She is a Lhasa Apso, with a long curly coat, the color of Devon cream and weights eighteen pounds.

Dr. Russo says it is a mystery to him that Rags has lived this long. But we know why. It is the love and devotion she receives from Mary, plus the fact that she knows how to find the sunny spots in life. She curls up in the front hall when the eastern sun pours through the glass door in the morning. She moves from room to room as the sun goes around the house, ending up by the kitchen window when the western sun reaches there in the afternoon. If you want to find Rags, just look for the sunny spot, and there she will be rolled up like a ball, basking away.

Rags' vision and hearing are almost gone. She no longer runs on those once fast moving legs. She has trouble with her hind quarters when she tries to get up from her favorite spot on a Persian rug. We lift her in and out of the car, holding her close in our arms. She still considers herself the protector and manages to bark now and then to keep up her role as guardian of her house.

The other day I took her down to the beach where she once loved to run on the hard sand, chasing seagulls, eyes sparkling as she reveled in the salty air and a quick dip in the water. Now she was content to gaze at the calm sea. After a few moments she sank down, laid her head on my knee and looked up. There were reflections of long and far away thoughts in her black eyes, of resignation and contentment, as if she were thinking of the transition that would close the chapter of our lives together.

And then, there is the village church nearby. The white clapboard edifice boasts no stained glass, no crystal spire, no gold-inlaid reredos. It is a simple church that sprang out of the rugged soil of the wilderness, erected by the strong hands of adventurous English settlers. As soon as they had a roof over their heads they built a house where they could meet with their God. I have bowed many times in this humble shrine during the years gone by.

The quiet haven ties me to the timeless. I don't have to be moved by a professional choir or a learned sermon. It is enough to just sit in this memory-laden sanctuary, to look out the mullioned glass windows at the old trees that shade the churchyard and listen to the birds pouring out gratitude to their creator. My anxiety ebbs and the tide of assurance slowly rises, lifting my spirit.

Tea for Two

One of nature's beneficent gifts to the human race is the tea leaf. This product from the Asian hills has spread cheer around the world. It has done more to create friendship and peace than armies and navies. The custom of tea drinking breaks down barriers of formality, warms the heart and relieves tension.

In my wanderings about the globe, so richly endowed with inviting tearooms, I have found no spot that can compare with my own hearthside. We do not compete with the British or the Japanese ritual but we thoroughly enjoy our own. Unlike lunch or dinner, there is little preparation and the main course is relaxation. I look forward to that half-hour on any afternoon. It is an oasis of refreshment when one's energy begins to lag.

Asiatics and Europeans alike have been captivated by the beverage called tea. The Chinese have been downing it for centuries in cups wihout handles, in palaces, pagodas and roadside tea stalls. They call it *cha*. The Russians call it *chi*, drinking it out of glasses so hot that you need gloves to handle them. The Japanese have developed their elaborate teahouse ritual, designed to rest body and mind through concentration on nature.

All work halts in England and all loyal citizens spread their bread with butter and their scones with jam and fill their cups for their tea time break. I have seen them pouring the sacred brew, seated on top of an iron sewer grate as the workers emerged from down below. The countryside abounds in tearooms with their festive offering of cakes and tarts.

I recall the Olympic Games held in London in 1948. It was a roaring hot day, well over ninety degrees, the highest temperature and humidity I ever experienced in England. As I watched the thrilling spectacle, coatless and thirsty, I dreamed of an ice cold drink. I buttonholed a vender who was serving the traditional cup of hot tea and made a plea for an iced drink. He grinned at me: "Nothing cold. This is England."

I exchanged churches and houses with an English friend one summer in attractive Mill Hill, northwest of London. It was a community full of wonderful folks. Along with the house, we inherited a maid named Beth and a friendly dog. The little corgi was a doll. So was Beth. The first morning she tapped on our bedroom door at seven. She whispered, "Here is your morning tea." We were thoroughly Anglicized within a fortnight.

We still talk about the elaborate tea we enjoyed with Bartelot cousins in Sussex, where they live on the soil given to our ancestor, Adam Bartelot, by William the Conqueror. And the next day, in the village of Bury nearby, we shared high tea with the novelist, John Galsworthy and his wife, Ada. He, too, belonged to the Bartelot clan. Then came tea parties in the Cotswolds, Devon and Cornwall, as we chugged around in our four cylinder Morris Cowley, which wheezed and coughed as we idled our way through the hedgerows and hills of that imcomparable countryside.

On another trip to the motherland, I was in the office of T. S. Eliot, where he worked directly with his publisher. It was originally a dignified old edifice in Russell Square, now badly beaten by German bombings. There was still a bit of dust around on top of the bookcases, desk and table. But the unperturbed poet was carrying on business as usual, working on a new play. He suggested tea after we had chatted for a while and produced some stoneware cups, cracked and beaten like the building. He rinsed them in the sink, filled a teapot from a steaming kettle, opened a bag of crumpets and set them on a table before us. He proposed a toast to the progress of English-American letters and fraternity among our people. It was a spontaneous gesture such as might occur when acquaintances are warmed by a cup of tea.

I once enjoyed tea with Stefan Zweig and his brilliant wife, Frederika, at their home on the Kapuzinerberg in Salzburg. This was before the last war. The atmosphere of the old mansion, the beautiful tea service and the Austrian dainties brought new friends together. They spoke of their writings and their efforts to correct the growing nationalistic barriers of Europe. The old hostilities were still in evidence — the chauvinistic emotion that was pushing people toward another conflict.

While living in China, I became an addict to the cherished herb of the Middle Kingdom. It was tea every day, all along the way. The sons of Han were sipping it in shops, buying it from pushcart venders on the street and from roadside dispensaries. When we took country trips, we always carried along a *qui hu,* which was a fast boiling tin pot that we could fill with water from a well or stream and boil for five full minutes before adding the tea leaves. This solved the problem of hygiene and our thirsty throats as well.

Today I laid one of our apple logs on the gooseneck andirons that stand like sentinels before the seventeenth century fireback, and then settled into the wing chair. I watched the flames licking up the chimney and thought of all the wood I had cut through the years. When age, disease or storm brought down one of our trees, I respectfully carried all usable remains to the barn or garage. There was no summary dismissal to the town dump. Those producers of blossoms, bird havens and our long-time companions, deserved deference. I cut them in eighteen inch lengths and stacked them in order — maple, oak, birch, cherry, pear, the cherished hard woods. I knew them by their bark and recalled when we planted them, those springs so long ago.

In due time, on some cool day, I would move them to the fireplace and lay them over a pile of old wood shingles and light a match. This would be the final parting after our many seasons together. The next day I would carry their ashes and spread them on the perennial bed, committing them to Mother Nature and the life cycle in which they had played a significant role.

There was a time when we did not use our best china and silver every day, but now every day is special and four o'clock tea is the high point. Sometimes Sue chooses the large silver tray and the silver Faneuil tea set, elegant in its simplicity and black ebony handles, with the pink luster cups and saucers or the Delecta plum and cherry cups. Today she used an antique tole tray, decorated in aqua and gold flowers, and placed on it the Imari tea set with the pheasant and peony that we bought in Japan fifty years ago.

People have different ways of making tea, but the ingredients are the same, namely *boiling* water, tea leaves, a good pot and a cozy to keep it hot. Many like their tea plain, which may be the connoisseur's choice but we were born and bred to a little bit of sugar and very light cream with ours. No blue-water-milk or lemon is allowed to desecrate our tea tray. We have a collection of teas on hand but our standbys are the good old English Breakfast, Darjeeling and Boston Harbor. We also enjoy Formosa Oolong and, of course, the jasmine flower tea, for its taste and aroma and the blossoms in the cup. We usually have an assortment of cookies in the crockery jar. We often have hot buttered scones with honey or small sandwiches. But our homemade bread, spread thinly with butter, is our favorite accompaniment to a cup of tea.

Tea parties, both large and small, have been an integral part of our lives, but "tea for two" is a celebration *extraordinaire.*

Togetherness in Nature

Beavers thrived in the Plymouth ponds in the days of the Pilgrims, providing pelts which the settlers shipped to London as payments on the loan that brought them to the New World. Bartlett Brook is called Beaver Dam Brook where it flows down from the cranberry bogs. The once plentiful beavers have been more or less eradicated in recent years. As expert builders of ponds and dams, these furry engineers ran into confrontations with trappers, farmers and bog owners and, needless to say, lost in the encounter.

One summer evening in northern Massachusetts, I stood on the bank of a beaver pond in the company of a native farmer who explained the close society operated by the amphibians. The colony had been in existence for several years. Beavers mate for life. As conscientious parents, they carry on an educational program for their offspring. They teach swimming, tree cutting and the storing of logs and bark for winter. They teach how to build an underwater home, designed to prevent a freeze up, with entrances and exits and a substantial overhead fortification against wolves and bears.

They run a modest engineering school, including elementary surveying necessary to choosing a dam site, the moving of stones and boulders, the art of applying mud to rocks and tree branches so as to form a lasting dam. I was impressed as I watched them working. There are many skills to learn in the beaver heritage. They have roots to establish and a way of life to master.

The elephants and baboons demand an even longer period of coexistence with their young. A more complex life style requires more tutelage, more mutuality. Most of the billions of creatures of land, sea and sky like company and have developed ways of living together for protection and companionship. Individual beasts and birds do not break home ties, turn vagabond and wander the counry "trying to find themselves." Dropouts seldom occur in nature. To split off is to perish. The instruction that shapes members of the animal kingdom is presented and absorbed, not through aloneness, but through being a learning member of the team.

Discipline is an imperative in the animal world. Training for survival is rigid. Obedience is required. The mother quail senses danger and calls to her offspring which hasten at once to her side.

Archibald Rutledge watched a gray fox lurking in the bushes along a rail fence, studying a brood of half grown turkeys as they fed with their mother. It was evening and the birds were tired and careless. The mother kept calling to them to be alert as they moved along the edge of the woods. One youthful gobbler started in pursuit of a grasshopper. The mother sounded an alarm. The fox crept forward through the grass, eyes gleaming, to cut the bird off from the flock. A few more steps and the turkey would have lost his life. The mother called again and the bird obeyed, turning and fleeing to her side. She gave a shrill cry of alarm and flew with her brood into the pine trees, out of reach of the enemy. Life was saved by obedience. The children of nature learn to obey.

Wild creatures are called upon daily to make life and death choices. They react with celerity. To defy a law of nature is to defy reason. Natural law and reason go hand-in-hand. The basic lessons in survival are passed on generation to generation through the association developed in nest, burrow, cave and jungle shelter.

My thoughts turn from the beavers to the lack of togetherness in America today. Divisiveness has become a national peril. Ethnic and minority groups create pandemonium, attacking all authority and one another. They scream "my rights" and "discrimination".

During the 1980 elections, a candidate for the presidency, speaking to a large ethnic convention, promised that if elected, he would make their language the second language of our country. We probably have fifty or more ethnic groups in our land. Can we teach fifty second languages in first grade?

When we became citizens, we pledged allegiance to the constitution of the United States. We became Americans. English is our national tongue. Privately we can study and speak all the languages we choose.

I recently heard on the radio an ethnic leader addressing his group. He declared that the objective of his people was to get "their share of the American pie." I was shocked at this low and self-seeking appeal. If we are split personalities, wrapped up in small packages of ethnic and linguistic ties, we will collapse like the Tower of Babel and the American dream will vanish. We must shake off the simplistic and destructive infatuation with polarization, with "my rights" and think more of the rights of others and the welfare of the whole.

And Still They Come

I never walk up or down the bulkhead steps of our cellar without thinking of Tony. He was six feet tall, rugged as the mountains of his native North Italy. He made me think of General Garibaldi, arousing his people to fight for freedom. The muscles of his shoulders and arms showed through a flimsy work shirt. His snapping brown eyes, black hair and curling moustache would captivate a portrait painter. He and his two sons had been digging out a bulkhead for our cellar and laying huge field stones for the steps.

"Why don't you take a breather, Tony?" I said. "I get a pain in my back just watching you shove those mammoth things around." Tony stood up, stretching his arms, saying, "This ain't bad. I am used to hard work. When I was twelve years old in Italy I worked in a gravel pit for fourteen cents a day, walkin' five miles each way in bare feet. We didn't have a clock. My father got up by the stars."

"I can hardly believe you, Tony," I interjected. "You are a miracle."

"I ran most of the way home nights, scared of the wild dogs that roamed the countryside. My father walked out part way to meet me."

162

His two boys leaned on their shovels and listened with due respect to their father, but with a mixture of pride and skepticism.

Tony lit a slender, twisted black cigar and continued: "We never ate meat, just mostly corn meal. My father worked part of the year on a farm. The rest of the time there was nothing to do. The money I earned helped keep us all from starvin'."

I thought of Governor Bradford's words which I had just read in his journal: "It is not by good and dainty fare, by peace and rest and heartsease in enjoying the contentments and good things of this world only, that preserve health and prolong life."

"How old were you, Tony, when you came over?" I asked.

"Fifteen," he said. "I started as a hod carrier and made more in one hour than I did in a day in Italy."

"Do you ever think of returning?"

Here Tony shook the ashes from his cigar and declaimed like an orator, gesticulating with both hands: "Not since I see that Statue of Liberty, *not once* have I want to go back. I tell my children how poor we were in the old country, but they don't beleef!" He drew a deep sigh and began again shifting the stones and showing the boys how to lay the mortar.

The sons, with their discipline in the work ethic, have measured up to Tony's standards. They are business men of highest caliber, active and respected citizens. One is the leading mason contractor and the other day I paid him $20.00 an hour to do a small job on our fireplace. I told him that if his father, to whom I paid ninety cents an hour in 1938 were living, he would surely exclaim: "I don't beleef!"

Another later Pilgrim who helped us restore our house, installing our plumbing and heating, was Gino. He also was from North Italy and came alone as a teenager. He was a skillful mechanic and genial company. During work breaks we often talked about politics, religion and music. He knew more about opera than I did and went to Boston or New York every winter to hear his favorites.

He said to me one day (with his head under the sink and a wrench in his hand) in one of our discussions on the state of the world, "There is only one America. All who come here can achieve an education and live as free people."

Gino made good in America, built up a successful business, was a member of town meeting and active in community affairs.

His three sons are scientists, holding important posts in our country.

The pilgrimage to America continues from north and south, east and west, year after year, by land, by sea, by air. People flee from hunger, povery and oppression to the one land they have dreamed about, with their worldly goods in a duffel bag, believing that here they can start over and build a new life.

There are those who would destroy the American dream. They ridicule our traditions. They tear down but construct nothing. They seek out our national shrines for defamation. They come to Plymouth. They spit on the Rock where the founders of New England disembarked. They arrange for television to broadcast their denunciations. But the Rock endures. All of the raging cannot move it. Neither the tirades of the cynics nor the storms of the sea can obliterate the dream of freedom generated here.

And still they come to America and to Plymouth Rock year in and year out, by the hundreds and by the thousands, in a never-ending pilgrimage. One of these very recent comers is Dr. Libor Brom, who emigrated from Czechoslovakia to discover that the American dream is still alive in spite of those who discount its health today. In a lecture at Hillsdale College he said:

> I believe there is a great difference between Americans and the people of other countries. Whenever I travel, I recognize this difference. These people have a dream, a sense that there exists a powerful force capable of leading the world to justice and peace. They are aware that there is a unique society in the world where God has put together all nationalities, races and interests of the globe for one purpose — to show the rest of the world how to live. The dream around the world, in spite of all contrary propaganda, is America.

Life Styles

Birds and beasts like to preen and primp and look their best. They follow the standards of their forebears but young humans tend to repudiate the etiquette of their parents. Our offspring do not carry on like colts, pups and birdlings. They break rules and defy tradition, increasingly so in recent decades.

Standards of youthful dress have imposed a rigid totalitarianism, requiring boys and girls to don the same faded blue jeans until they look like Maoist ants. They deprive their elders, as well as themselves, of ever seeing a pretty leg or a lovely bust. The sweep of the proletariat forces all into one blurred block of impersonality. Male and female have been swallowed up in a dull collage.

Now take Candy. She likes to look stunning. She enjoys being brushed and is proud of her glossy, golden coat. She will go, heel, stay and sit, conforming happily to the discipline of training. She is ever ready to enter a beauty competition.

We never saw our granddaughter, Sarah, in a dress until she was sixteen years old and that was a reluctant concession to her grandmother's birthday party. She preferred blue jeans, layered shirts, jackets and things. But she spent three hours bathing, brushing and grooming her sixteen and a half hands jumper, Lovely Sides, for her weekly horse show in Vermont, then three more hours braiding her mane and tail in the fanciest of designs. What a paragon of beauty Lovely Sides was as she stepped into the ring. And Sarah, too, in her highly polished boots, her natty white breeches, monogrammed white turtle neck blouse, navy blue riding jacket, neatly styled hair under a natty cap and white gloves!

The onlookers and fans could defy dress standards and loll about on the grass and bleachers in anything they wished but not the riders and the winners. They were dressed to the hilt. And Sarah came off with a blue ribbon every time. The next day, however, getting her into a simple skirt and blouse for church was a blue ribbon achievement for her parents. This was somewhat of a puzzle to me.

One seldom sees a frowsy deviate in the avian world. We catch our breath at the sight of a cardinal or an oriole. But the Hippies paraded barefoot and were proud of their matted hair. My college generation was characterized for its follies and foibles, but we did set a record for style with our plus-fours, wool golf stockings, cordovan shoes, button down shirts, rep ties, Shetland jackets and gray flannels.

Even my son's generation at Yale held on pretty well, minus the Norfolk jackets and knickers. But the Hippies changed all that. They initiated the unwashed and unkempt look. During this period, while lecturing at Harvard, I dined with the students in their beautiful English style refectory. The boys wore no ties, no jackets, even for dinner. The era of iconoclasm had banished the tweeds and the Shetlands. Jeans were in, jackets were out, along with rep ties and button downs. This was the low tide when Soviet students sent clothing packages to Ivy League undergraduates, having read of their patched and fringed jeans.

But finally the beat generation got tired of hating the establishment. Hatred takes a lot out of one even when it seems justifiable. They also wearied of looking at each other in dismal rags and began to embrace some of the amenities they had scorned. Maybe they had taken a few notes from nature's book on how to get ahead. Like Candy, perhaps, they recognized that good grooming attracts friends, or sensed, like Lovely Sides, that style is the way to win a blue ribbon, or that the cardinal and the oriole contribute a little more gaiety to life than the grackle and the crow.

For some time now, a change has been in evidence. There are the Preppies who opted for corduroys over patched jeans. They began taking more pride in their grades and looking more favorably on business and Ivy League schools.

Ronny cut our lawn for several summers while in high school. We paid him in dollar bills as a rule, which he would roll up and stuff in the pocket of his jeans. I always scolded him, saying he would surely lose his money and once offered him an old wallet of mine. But no thank you. Wallets were out. But last fall when I paid him, he displayed a wallet. He was off for college now and had learned that the once discarded Wall Street symbol is back in favor with his peers.

Now the Ruggies are the new pace-setters. Shirts with alligators and bears on them are obsolete. Socks and athletic shoes are in. No more bare feet. Good manners are more popular. Dressing up for parties is alright. Jobs are important.

Sarah is now in an Ivy League college and wears pretty dresses and smart hair styles. Her brother, Ben, in a traditional preparatory school, no longer fights jackets and ties. Girls, especially, are paying more attention to good grooming. They may be noticing the beauty contest going on among our female newscasters. Rouge, lipstick, silk stockings and fetching hair-dos are coming back. The plain Janes with stringy hair and granny glasses are passé. A society of pretty girls and handsome boys just might set the bull market soaring.

The Brook and the Bog

I suppose everyone in the world loves a babbling brook, Our brook comes flowing down from the ponds to the west of us into Bartlett Pond, which empties into the ocean. It isn't boisterous but it is never still, always gently rippling along. Its narrow bridge offers rails to lean against and gaze up or down stream at the tremulous reflections of willow tendrils, alders and wild roses that line its banks, and at the deep blue of the sky with its white puffs and mounds of cumulus clouds. It is some comfort to us that our house sets on a gently rising hill about 300 feet from the brook. We are never bothered by water in our cellar as some of our neighbors are. Nor did we have to constantly watch our young children. We owned a rowboat which they enjoyed with us.

Our ten year old son, Bob, had a friend, Myles Standish Sampson (twelfth generation), who spent summers with his grandmother, Mazie Sampson, on the other side of the brook. She kept an eagle eye on the boys. "Don't go near that Reamy bog," was her first order of the season, "It has quicksand and it will suck you right down."

The bog was a musky, matted swamp of decayed vegetable

matter, wet and spongy. It evolved from a small pond of about half an acre in size and was the scary place in our neighborhood. No one knew the whole history of it, but one thing for sure, it was to be avoided. Cat-tails, skunk cabbage, ferns, wild butterfly bushes and a jungle of impenetrable brush formed the outer edges. Farther from the perimeter, on a damp slope, were masses of purple loosestrife, easily seen from the road. Years ago, a barbed-wire fence had been placed around it, of which only a few broken remnants remain.

Mazie liked to tell how her father's bull calf had wandered into the bog and never came out. Neighbors tried to help but no one could reach the poor thing. His moos and the tinkle of his bell wrung their hearts, but they could only let the creature sink until the bell was silent and he was gone forever. The boys' hair stood on end at this horror story and they retold it to everyone who would listen, with their own embellishments.

Mazie was a loyal, warm-hearted neighbor and invaluable assistance in the restoration of our house and in researching Plymouth history. Once a week she called and said, "Our car is going over the Pine Hills this morning. Anything you need in town?" Those were the days of gasoline rationing stamps. To save a gallon of gas was as critical then as it is now, although for a different reason. We were fighting a war. All window shades were drawn at sundown and our cars crept through the Pine Hills with blinders on their headlights.

Mazie was a Pilgrim descendant, a Daughter of the American Revolution, the village historian and a storehouse of information on local lore. Powder Hill, where the Revolutionary War soldiers hid their powder, was just back of her house and their drilling ground was the triangular field at the end of our road. The Cape Cod house, beyond her place, was once a tavern on the King's Highway, as the road was then called. It was a narrow, winding dirt road, hugging the coastline from Plymouth to Sandwich. She knew the book and page in the Town Records that tell how Joseph Bartlett, then living in our house, March 5, 1667, was fined three shillings four pence for striking an Indian. I was impressed that the Pilgrims had laws on their books to protect Indians.

But Mazie had an ever-watchful concern for her grandson's safety. The boy could not ride a bicycle because cars came so seldom down our road that he would forget to watch, she said. He could not wade in the brook for fear of falling on a slippery stone. He would surely drown if he swam in the ocean. Her admonitions about the dangers of ponds, streams, ocean, climbing trees, woods and just about everything that boys hanker to do, did not, however, deter them from occasional escapades.

To get into our rowboat was forbidden, but Mazie did consent one day, after much cautioning about hooks, to let Myles fish with Bob from the brook bridge since she could observe them from her living room window. But she fell asleep in the rocking chair while reading birthday letters and cards.

Our telephone rang. It was Mazie's excited voice: "The boys are gone. I dozed for a moment." She had run down to the brook, she said, and there on the ground, at the edge of the bridge, were two poles, the lines neatly wrapped about them, but no boys. Mazie was hysterical. They had been kidnapped! They had been drowned and were floating down the brook to Bartlett Pond! They had run away!

We called our neighbors, but no one had seen them. Sue stayed by the telephone. She checked Geller's Garage, where one could buy ice-cream cones and bubble gum, and Lucy's Fruit Stand. The boys had not been at either place.

By now Sue and I were getting concerned ourselves. Paul Clark rowed our boat down the brook to the pond and back, but reported no clues. Others joined me and we scoured woods and fields, calling until we were hoarse. Some one had notified the police and a patrol car came wailing up and down the road, stopping to ask us questions. Had we noticed any strange car in the area or any magazine peddlers? We had not. The police took off for the highway to make further inquiries.

Then Mazie screamed: "The bog! They're in the bog!" We rushed down the road, puffing and panting and scrambled over the banking, stumbling down the hill, and came face to face with two startled boys, with arms full of beautiful purple loosestrife. Their shoes were wet and muddy, their faces and hands sweaty and streaked with dirt, but they were exuberant and smiling.

"Happy Birthday, Grandmother," Myles said as he gave her the flowers.

Mazie was completely disarmed and could not say a word. She

took the gift in one arm and hugged her grandson with the other. Then she sat down on the hillside, exhausted. We breathed a long sigh of relief. That they had ventured off bounds into the bog area was an issue to be discussed later.

An Age-old Covenant

Long, long ago, in the far off days when man and dog came together, a covenant of loyalty developed, man agreeing to feed and pet dog, and dog promising to guard and serve man. This ancient compact is laden with memories of romantic association between the human and the animal world. This epic of fidelity, upheld by these faithful creatures, brightens the somber pages of history with annals of devotion.

The dog volunteered to dwell with man centuries ago, to enter his home, not as a servant, but as a companion, to share his quarters, eat his food, listen to his conversation and enter into his joys and sorrows. It is a unique covenant. Literature is rich with stories of undying friendships. Man, more often than beast, may have failed to keep the covenant.

This friend is never too weary to walk beside the plowman, to cock his ears while dozing, alert to the slightest alien sound, to come when his name is whispered to sit by one's side. Many of us know the rewards of fellowship with such a colleague, brightening lonely moments, finding comfort in that ever-welcome presence.

Candy is close to perfection according to retriever standards,

Tenants in Common

The other day I was making a demographic survey of our spot of earth that has been in the Bartlett family for 324 years, generation after generation passing on the title to a successor in the same blood line.

Most of those who lived on the homestead before me have been buried in the churchyard close to the small, white framed meeting-house, a few hundred feet or so from our back yard. It has a balcony running around three sides of the sanctuary and the original boxed-in pews. A hill with sandy soil, good drainage and sufficient number of shade trees seems an ideal spot for a burial ground. The oldest headstones are lichen covered and difficult to read. But one can make out scores of Bartletts and a goodly number of Holmes and Clarks.

People have built graveyards, I suppose, to affirm their yearning for immortality, the hope that continuity will persist between the dead and the living, that the title to ownership will remain unbroken. A sturdy oak watches over our family lot, close to the comforting presence of the church, and a *catawbiensis alba* rhodo-dendron. The huge cluster of orchid-like blossoms, throats speckled with gold, open pink-flushed, turning to pure white. In May, Sue and I added two *Kaempferi* azaleas and a pink dogwood, watering them all summer. Flowers have been such an inherent part of our lives that we cannot imagine resting in peace without their benediction above us.

I took a walk through the churchyard this November day. The bronze and red oak leaves were gliding down onto the cooling earth. The autumn birds were taking their posts in the bare arms of the oaks — the cheery chickadees, the gray-clad juncos and the white-breasted nuthatches. They are ready to patrol the woodlands and keep guard over the sleeping earth until spring stirs branch and blade to new life.

My land abounds in birds and animals. They have been tenants in common with me for nearly fifty years. Their names are written in the Book of Nature in records that prove they were here. Their descendants today animate the place. This assemblage includes squirrels, chipmunks, rabbits, foxes, raccoons, skunks, muskrats, deer, gulls, ducks, geese, grouse, quail, pheasant, kingbirds, phoebes, swallows, robins, song sparrows, orioles, frogs, peepers, turtles, cicadas, katydids, crickets, grasshoppers, bees, wasps and butterflies.

The land has been theirs by common use for centuries. Before the Indians, before the Vikings, before the Pilgrims, before the foot of *Homo sapiens* was planted on this beautiful terrain, it was theirs to glory in.

Birds and animals do not establish cemeteries for themselves. They leave behind them no legal documents, no wills or codicils to guide their descendants, only traditions like playing together, hunting together, drinking gratefully at a stream or pond, the joy of eating, relaxing in the sun, saluting dawn and sunset with a lilt of song or a squeal of happiness.

At winter's demise, turtles, frogs and peepers will emerge with honey bees and the winged creatures, returning from the southland, to enliven the scene. The dormant trees will feel the kindling of life until their jeweled buds brighten the landscape. Forsythia, lilac, bridal wreath and rhododendron will break forth with the annunciation of immortality.

Once again the churchyard and the environs will be alive with

the normal population of birds, beasts and insects. Without any legal agreements on file in the registry of deeds, their pattern of life will unfold in its timeless way. Bees will fertilize the fruit orchard, butterflies and hummingbirds care for the flowers. Gulls will scavenge beaches and dumps and earthworms improve the soil. The swallows will clear the air of insects and woodpeckers protect the forest. Tree foliage will purify the atmosphere and blueberry bushes will offer shelter for the robin's nest.

I walked home the back way through the woods and came upon a colony of blue gentians at the edge of the pasture, the first I had seen, bravely blooming in the nippy air. Their golden eyes caught the last rays of the sun as autumn chill spread its warning over the landscape. The sky-blue loveliness made me determine to come back in the spring and move a small company to the south side of the barn where they would spread in front of the silvery shingles and we could reap a bonus of beauty when all the gardens were bare.

A Weatherbeaten Face

Winters can be rugged in Plymouth with sharp winds and rough seas but snow storms generally are lighter than inland because of the salt water. Last winter we experienced a memorable snowfall. Our house was built back from the exposure of the ocean, behind a hill for protection. The gambrel roof offered a squatty resistance to the wind. The gunstock beams at the corners, the rafters and joices of oak have carried it through many blows.

A gray sky and cursory flakes gave us warning to settle in. I contemplated our needs, brought in kindling and firewood, piled it by the fireplaces and on the cellar landing. I locked the barn and toolshed doors, after locating the snow shovel and the rock salt to spread on the brick terrace. I ran the car into the garage and pulled down the big door.

The temperature stood at twenty-six degrees with the wind from the northeast. I could feel the storm coming. We stocked the bird feeder with ground corn and sunflower seeds. The juncos and chickadees seemed to come from everywhere. Candy had made her walking tour of the place and was waiting patiently outside the kitchen door. She was too mannerly to scratch or bark like uneducated canines. She knew we would open it for her.

The three of us relaxed before an oak fire. Twilight was creeping in. The snow flakes grew larger. The house was snug with partially insulated walls (by us during our restoration), with aluminum storm doors and windows instead of the old-fashioned wooden ones (after long debate) and a modern forced hot air heating system, supplemented by three fireplaces.

What luxury when compared with Robert Bartlett's first home! The Pilgrims, who survived in those hastily built cottages in 1621 amid the howling winds and drifting snow, would have considered our house a utopian creation. How cold our bedrooms must have been even in 1660. We have a soapstone foot warmer and a long handled, copper bed warmer, that was filled with hot coals from the fireplace and whisked about between the frigid sheets.

William Bradford gave us a picture of the winter environs when they landed:

> And for the season it was winter, and they that know the winters of that country know them to be sharp and violent, and subject to cruel and fierce storms, dangerous to travel to known places, much more to search an unknown coast. Besides, what could they see but a hideous and desolate wilderness. For summer being done all things stand upon them with a weatherbeaten face, and the country, full of woods and thickets, presented a wild and sage hue. If they looked behind them, there was a mighty ocean, which they had passed and was now a main bar and gulf to separate them from all the civil parts of the world. What could now sustain them but the Spirit of God and His grace?

The hardships of the Pilgrims continued through the years, not only in combating the ravages of the elements, but struggling with economic problems, disease, loneliness and disappointment. Many of their relatives and friends had been unable to join them as planned. John Robinson, their beloved spiritual leader in Holland, died suddenly before he could cross over. The Pilgrim band was devastated with grief.

Governor Bardford reported in his journal:

> It is a marvel it did not wholly discourage and sink them.

But they gathered up their spirits, and the Lord so helped them, whose work they had in hand, as now when they were at lowest ebb, they began to rise again, and being stripped in a manner of all human helps and hopes, He brought things about otherwise in his divine providence.

When their bulwark, Elder William Brewster, who was raised in a cultured family and served in the court of Queen Elizabeth, died at age seventy-seven, Bradford recorded some of the privations he had endured.

He was willing to bear his burthen with the rest, living many times without bread or corn many months together, having many times nothing but fish and often wanting that also; and drunk nothing but water for many years together, yea till within five or six years of his death.

People of will and faith, they survived their wilderness existence with no outside support. And here we were facing a mild reproduction of a Plymouth blizzard, with electric lights, oil heat, snow plows, warm clothes and plenty of good food.

Before climbing into our poster bed, I peered out the window at the street light on the road. It was surrounded by a dense veil of snow flakes. The wind was abating. The snow was falling in thick curtains, enfolding the house. In bed I could feel the silence. There was no sound on the blanketed roadway, no sign yet of plow or passing vehicle. A new world was evolving about me—of quiet and repose. The weary earth seemed to be resting peacefully after expending its full energy in spring and summer.

With the tranquil snowfall, I slept late the next morning. I wakened to see scattered flakes still falling from the thinning clouds. About ten o'clock the sun burst through, as by a magician's wand, creating a wonderland of glittering trees, roof tops, lawn and field. It was one of those rare storms—no zero temperatures, no howling winds, no high drifts, no soggy downfall—one of winter's dramatic feats.

Crystalline brilliance pervaded the outside world. A downy woodpecker in the Norway maple was trying to evaluate the situation, lodged precariously on a twig end. It was puzzled by the white mantle that covered the once familiar tree. There was no place to land and start drilling for breakfast. A rabbit, crouched along the front hedgerow, was timid about starting across the yard. It needed longer legs to cope with the snow.

Candy was out with me, taking a look at the strange overnight transformation. She plunged into the fluffy mass, with a happy bark, emerging with a coat covered with diamonds, her eyes dancing at what was an exciting adventure for her. With boots on, I waded around the house in the twelve inch snow, pleased that the storm had dealt gently with us. I was amazed by the vista that nature had produced. The place, in its many changing, seasonal moods had never looked more enchanting.

I shoveled a path to the garage, put out some suet for the hungry woodpecker, shook the snow off our prized English box-wood that guards our front door and cleared the walk and steps leading to the road. Bud Fuller waved from the town plow as he flung the snow up against our stone wall.

Candy and I could smell the baked beans and codfish cakes. We stomped the snow from our feet and announced we were ready for lunch, which Sue had set on the small tavern table in front of the fireplace. Above the mantel hung a framed copy of the hand written will of Robert Bartlett, the man who built my house, with a complete inventory of all his possessions when he died. Town Records show that he was an active citizen, a cooper and carpenter, surveyor of roads and a highway engineer. He served as a juror, a member of the Grand Jury and the Grand Inquest. He built a bridge over Eel River and helped form a neighborhood protection group to function in time of danger.

He owned land near Duxbury, in Dartmouth, in Punckateesett "over against Rhode Island," as well as in Eel River and Manomet. Robert had his hands full with his substantial acreage, two dwellings, at Eel River and Bartlett Brook (our house), cattle, horses, barns and a lively family of eight children.

Although a member of the meetinghouse, Robert criticized the monotonous psalm singing of the congregation. Perhaps he missed the organ and choir that he had enjoyed as a boy in the Church of England. The Town Records state that on May 1, 1660:

Att this Court, Robert Bartlett appeered, being summoned to answere for speakeing contemptously of the ordinance of singing psalms, and was convict of the fact and did in part acknowlidg his evill therein on which the Court sharply admonished him, and required that he should acknowlidg his falt, which hee engaged to do as hee should bee minded of them, and soe hee was discharged.

However, Robert was on good terms with his pastor. The Reverend John Cotton visited him during his final illness and witnessed his last will and testament.

974.4
Bartlett, Robert Merrill
My corner of New England

Dues for the Cotuit Library
Association, if you wish to join,
are $2.00 to 5.00 for an in-
dividual and 6.00 to 10.00 for
a family.

If you have a home computer with
internet access you may:

- request an item be placed on hold
- renew an item that is overdue
- view titles and due dates checked out
  on your card
- view your own outstanding fines

To view your patron record from
your home computer:
Click on the NSPL homepage:
http://nspl.suffolk.lib.ny.us

North Shore Public Library ·